T-34
MEDIUM TANK
(1939-1943)

MIKHAIL BARYATINSKIY

Ian Allan
PUBLISHING

First published 2007

ISBN (10) 0 7110 3265 3
ISBN (13) 978 0 7110 3265 1

All rights reserved. No part of this book may be reproduced or transmitted in any form or by any means, electronic or mechanical, including photocopying, recording or by any information storage and retrieval system, without permission from the Publisher in writing.

© Mikhail Baryatinskiy 2007

Published by Ian Allan Publishing

an imprint of Ian Allan Publishing Ltd, Hersham, Surrey KT12 4RG.
Printed by Ian Allan Printing Ltd, Hersham, Surrey KT12 4RG.

Code: 0707/B2

Visit the Ian Allan Publishing web site at:
www.ianallanpublishing.com

Design concept and layout by Polygon Press Ltd. (Moscow, Russia).
Coloured illustrations by A.Aksenov.

This book is illustrated with photos from the personal collections of M. Baryatinsky, A. Aksenov and M. Kolomyets.

Translation by N. Vladimov.

Cover illustrations.
Front cover:
A T-34 made by Krasnoye Sormovo in position. 2nd Baltic Front, 1945.

Back cover:
Above: A T-34 tank mod. 1942 with improved turret in the exposition of the Great Patriotic War Museum in Moscow.

Below: A T-34 tank mod. 1942 during the Tankman Day celebration in Kubinka. 10 September 2005.

Tanks of the 4th Guards Kantemirovskaya Tank Division in Gorky Street before the military parade. Moscow, 7 November 1945. A T-34 mod. 1943 heads the formation.

A T-34 in front of the Volgograd Tractor Works (formerly known as the Stalingrad Tractor Works).

Contents

TANK DEVELOPMENT HISTORY

HOW IT ALL STARTED

During an enlarged meeting of the State Defence Committee on 4 May 1938, with Vyacheslav Molotov in the chair and Joseph Stalin, Klement Voroshilov, other top military and political leaders of the country, representatives of the national defence industry, and commanding officers of tank units who had just returned from Spain, a baseline schematic diagram of the new wheel-cum-track tank, the BT-20, was presented, drafted at the Komintern Locomotive Plant in Kharkov. The new design sparked a storm of debate over the suitability of the wheel-and-track running gear in current tanks.

Those who had just seen combat in Spain, including A.A.Vetrov and D.G. Pavlov (the latter was head of the Automobile and Armour Directorate (AAD) at that moment) had very different standpoints on the subject. The heated polemics left the opponents of the wheel-cum-track chassis in the minority, for they referred to the allegedly faulty operation of BT-5 tanks during the war in Spain, which was actually not a valid argument for as few as 50 such tanks saw combat in Spain. Also invalid were their references to the low reliability of the running gear, because in September 1937 no significant breakdowns were reported during a 500-km road march on wheels to the Aragon front, and only a year and a half later BT-7 tanks of the 6th Tank Brigade undertook an even longer, 800-km, march to Kalkin-Gol on tracks without any failures.

It is most likely that it was not the reliability, but the very need to have wheel-cum-track chassis on contemporary tanks that mattered: wheels were intended for high-speed marches on good paved roads, which was a fairly rare pleasure.

Was it really worth making the tank design so very intricate? Whereas the BT-7's chassis was not very complicated, in the BT-20 with three pairs of driven road wheels the running gear turned out to be excessively tricky. There must have been some other explanations of industrial, operational and political natures as well: if the top brass had an affection for the wheel-cum-track design, why disagree?

But let's backtrack to the BT-20's history in order to clarify some points, essential because this particular vehicle was the prototype of the tank later referred to as the T-34.

The fact is that in 1937 Plant No. 183 (the Kharkov steam-engine works was renamed in the late-1936) was tasked to develop the BT-7IS and BT-9 wheel-and-track tanks to meet the requirements specified by the Automobile and Armour Directorate. Moreover, it was planned to build 100 BT-7IS tanks that year. The KB-109 design bureau of Department 100 (the tank production division of the plant), headed by Mikhail I. Koshkin, failed to do the job, and moreover Koshkin did his best to delay the work of the group of engineers headed by Military Engineer 3rd Rank Adolf Ya. Dik, an adjunct of the Stalin Military Mechanisation and Motorisation Academy, who had been sent to the plant to draft designs of what was going to be the BT-IS tank.

On 28 September 1937 the plant Director I.P. Bondarenko received the following instructions from his immediate superiors:

"To Director of Plant No. 183. Pursuant to Government Resolution No. 94ss dated 15 August 1937 the AAD was tasked to draft, build experimental vehicles and put into mass-production a fast tank with synchronized wheel-cum-track chassis. Whereas the task is critical and the deadlines set by the Government are tough, the 8th Main Directorate (of the People's Commissariat of the Defence Industry) authorises you to organize the work as follows:

1. establish a separate design bureau, directly subordinate to the Plant Chief Engineer, to develop the vehicle.

2. as agreed with Automobile and Armour Directorate and the Stalin Military Mechanisation and Motorisation Academy, appoint Military Engineer 3rd Rank Adolf Ya. Dik, an adjunct of the above Academy, as head of the newly formed design bureau and assign 30 pre-graduation officer-cadets of the academy to the bureau from 5 October, and another 20 from 1 December.

3. as agreed with the Automobile and Armour Directorate of the Workers and Peasants' Red Army, appoint Captain Yegeny A. Kulchitsky as Chief Consultant.

4. no later than 30 September, assign the eight best tank designers of the plant to be heads of working groups, and appoint a standard compliance officer, a secretary and a record keeper.

5. establish a mock-up and pattern shop at the design bureau and create priority conditions at all workshops of the plant for the design and development process under the new project.

6. develop three running gear versions and build two experimental vehicles as approved.

7. agree development issues with the Automobile and Armour Directorate no later than 15 October 1937."

As a result, a more powerful design bureau was created at the plant than the one it had had.

The Automobile and Armour Directorate vested the development of the new tank at the Kharkov plant in Captain Ye.A. Kulchitsky, Military Engineer 3rd Rank A.Ya. Dik, a group of engineers and 41 officer-cadets of the Military Mechanisation and Motorisation Academy. The plant in turn assigned its 22 best specialists for the job.

Adolf Dik was appointed the head of the design bureau, while Engineer P.N. Goryunov became his Assistant and Captain Kulchitsky was nominated the AAD consultant. V.M. Doroshenko was made the program manager for the driver's compartment, M.I. Tarshinov was responsible for the hull and engineer Gorbenko for the engine. The transmission and the running gear were assigned to A.A. Morozov and P.P. Vasilyev respectively.

The requirements for the new BT-20 wheel-cum-track combat vehicle were specified by the AAD on 13 October 1937 as follows:

"Requirements to the new BT-20 wheel-cum-track tank

1. Type – wheel-cum-track, 6-wheel drive, Christie-type.

2. Combat weight – 13-14 tonnes.

3. Armament – 1x45 mm 3 DT gun and a self-defence flame-thrower, or 1x76 mm 3 DT gun and a flame-thrower. Every 5th tank must have an anti-aircraft machinegun mount.

4. ammunition load carried – 2,500 – 3,000 MG 130-150x45 mm or 50x76 mm rounds.

5. Armour: front – 25 mm, conical turret – 20 mm, sides, rear – 16 mm, roof, bottom – 10 mm. The armour should be all sloped, with a min angle of 18 deg for the slanted hull and turret plates.

An experimental A-30 wheel-cum-track vehicle during tests at the Kubinka proving ground. 1939.

An A-20 tank during field trials. 1939.

6. Speed – the same for track and wheel running gear: max 70 km/h, min 7 km/h.

7. Crew – 3.

8. Cruising range – 300-400 km.

9. Engine – BD-2 developing 400-600 hp.

10. Transmission – BT-IS wheel-cum-track type (driving power when on wheels taken from steering clutches).

11. Suspension – independent; torsion bars preferable over carriage springs.

12. Orion stabilizer and turret traverse stabilizer by engineer Povalov; searchlight for night firing, reaching out to 1,000 m.

No information about the group of designers led by Adolf Dik is available after November 1937, but it is known for sure that the BT-20 requirements were specified to a large extent based on the design solutions proposed by the team in summer 1937 including the design of reduction gears, the sloped hull roof, the lateral driveshafts of the wheels and the slanted carriage springs. Yet another proposal by Dik's team to use five pairs of road wheels for better load distribution was also approved, though in vehicles well after the BT-20.

It is astonishing that there are no references to the special design bureau in the publications concerning the T-34's development history. What they hold are brief hightlights about a plant division or an experimental design bureau headed by A.A. Morozov, but with almost the same staff of specialists as mentioned above. Moreover, the brochure published on the occasion of the 70th anniversary of the Kharkov-based Morozov engineering design bureau reads that it was M.I. Koshkin who organized the KB-24 design bureau in order to develop the new wheel-cum-track tank as directed by the AAD. It also says that he selected designers from volunteers of the KB-190 and KD-35 design bureaus (the latter supporting mass-production of the heavy T-35 tank at that time).

The fate of the separate design bureau must have been quite unenviable, with a wave of arrests unleashed onto the plant in the autumn 1937 and spring 1938. Plant Director Bondarenko was sent to prison, sentenced to death and executed by firing squad. Many other designers and workers of the plant cast their lot with him. For instance, Chief Engineer F.I. Lyashch was arrested on charges of rendering machines ineffective; also Chief Metallurgist A.M. Metantsev and many others, who had allegedly been "hooked" by the "evil" director of the plant, were persecuted, accused of almost all the sins imaginable from "lack of vigilance" to "organization of an explosion at the plant..."Very many skilful and talented specialists were repressed: former chief of the tank design bureau A.O. Firsov was arrested in March 1937, followed by chief of the diesel department K.F. Chelpan and many others at the year-end.

This is probably the main reason why the design diagram of the BT-20 was never drafted until mid-March 1938, meaning one and a half months' delay. The diagram was approved by the AAD on 25 March that year, and then brought to the attention of the Defence Committee at the aforesaid meeting. No resolution was made in support of either of the two types of running gear at that meeting, but the minutes of a meeting of the Defence Committee, which was devoted to the Red Army's arms program, included the following line: "The suggestion by Comrade Pavlov to assign Plant No. 183 to develop a tracked only tank is approved as reasonable, for it allows increasing the front armour to 30 mm. The turret should be adjusted to accommodate a 76-mm gun. The crew shall be four men…Approved unanimously." Still there were no official decisions at the very top level, which gave the AAD leadership the opportunity to push through a modified list of requirements for the BT-20 wheel-cum-track tank. For the tank to withstand hits by 12.7-mm armour-piercing bullets, the armour of the hull and the turret was made thicker and the armour plates became even more sloped than before. The weight of the vehicle was set at 16.5 tonnes, so it was now more a medium tank than a light one. The crew was four-men, and the armament was the same, only with the flame thrower removed.

WHEELS OR TRACKS?

In August 1938, the USSR Defence Committee issued a resolution on tank armament which contained a requirement to develop new types of tanks in less than one year – by July 1939 – with weapons, armour and mobility matching future wars.

In early September 1938 the sketch and the mock-up of the BT-20 tank were submitted for consideration of the AAD commission headed by Military Engineer 1st rank Ya.L. Skvirsky. The commission approved the project, but tasked the design bureau and Plant No. 183 to develop and build one wheel-cum-track tank with a 45-mm gun and two tracked tanks with 76-mm guns.

This means that the tracked design was not in the least an initiative of the plant, but an official requirement of the Automobile and Armour Directorate of the Red Army! The facts presented here contradict the legend, cultivated for over half a century, that the new tank design was the result of the engineering and strategic creativity of Koshkin (who, by the way, got his degree as an engineer merely three years prior to the events under discussion) who was allegedly developing the new tank almost illegally and very often in harsh conditions.

In October 1938 the plant sent the drawings and the mock-ups of the two tanks developed in line with the directives of the AAD – the A-20 wheel-cum-track and the A-20G fully-tracked vehicles. These were inspected by the Supreme Military Council of the Red Army on 9 and 10 December 1938, and approved on 27 February 1939 by the USSR Defence Committee. Afterwards the plant received an order for test versions of A-20 and A-32 (the new factory designation for the A-20G).

As there was little time to make all the drawings, the need arose to involve more designers in the project. In the early 1939 three tank-oriented design bureaus of Plant No. 183 – namely

An A-20 wheel-cum-track tank climbing slopes on wheels. Kubinka proving ground, 1939.

A-20 and A-32

The vehicles' characteristics during the trials were as follows.

COMPARATIVE CHARACTERISTICS OF A-20 AND A-32 TANKS		
	A-20	**A-32**
Combat weight, kg	18,000+-200	19,000+-200
Crew	4	4
Length, mm	5,760	5,760
Width, mm	2,650	2,730
Height on wheels, mm	2,411	2,411
Height on tracks, mm	2,435	2,435
Height on tracks without turret, mm	1,538	1,538
Track gauge, mm	2,250	2,300
Distance between hubs of drive sprocket and idler, mm	5,060	5,060
Distance between hubs of first and last road wheels, mm	3,511	3,590
Ground clearance, mm	400 – 410	385 – 400
Armour, mm:		
hull front	20/sloped at 56°	20/sloped at 56°
sides	25/sloped at 90°	30/sloped at 90°
rear	16/sloped at 45°	16/sloped at 45°
roof and bottom	10	10
turret sides	25/sloped at 25°	25/sloped at 25°
turret roof	10	10
Armament	1x45 mm, 2 DT machineguns	1x76 mm, 2 DT machineguns
Ammunition load:		
rounds	152	72
machinegun magazines	43	26
Engine	V-2, initial series	
Max horsepower	500 at 1,800 rpm	
Specific horsepower	450 at 1,750 rpm	
Top speed on tracks, km/h:		
road	74.7	74.7
off-road	57	65

KB-190, KB-35 and KB-24 – were united into a single team, code-named Section 520. The experimental and test workshops also merged and M.I. Koshkin was appointed Chief Designer of Section 520, while A.A. Morozov was nominated the head of the design bureau and deputy chief designer and N.A. Kucherenko became his deputy.

In May 1939 the first two vehicles were assembled to undergo factory trials in Kharkov before their field tests, lasting from 17 July to 23 August. The test report reads that neither of them was equipped properly. This was true in relation to the A-32, which had no OPVT deep-wading snorkel and no ZIP tools and accessories kit mounted. Moreover six of its road wheels were borrowed from a BT-7, whose wheels were a little narrower, and the stowage arrangements were far from good.

As for the distinctions of the two experimental vehicles, the test commission concluded as follows: the A-32 had no wheel-driven chassis, its armour was 30 mm thick unlike the 25-mm armour of its rival, it had a 76-mm L-10 gun instead of a 45-mm gun as its main armament, and weighed 19 tons fully loaded. The front of the tank's interior and its sides were adjusted to stow 76-mm rounds. Due to the absence of the wheel drive, and its five road wheels, the interior layout of the A-32 was slightly different from that of the A-20. As for other mechanisms and systems, the two had no significant differences.

The A-20 covered 872 km during the factory tests, of which 655 km were on tracks and 217 on wheels, while the A-32's record was only 235 km. After the field test phase, the A-20 had a mileage of 3,267 km, of which 2,176 were on tracks, while the A-32 covered only 2,886 km.

Colonel V.N. Chernyayev, who was the chairman of the test commission, did not give preference to either of the two vehicles, so which was better remained unclear.

An experimental A-32 medium tank prototype during tests at a proving ground in summer 1939.

On 23 September 1939 the military chiefs of the Red Army watched a demonstration of armoured vehicles, with K.Ye. Voroshilov, A.A. Zhdanov, A.I. Mikoyan, N.A. Voznesensky, D.G. Pavlov and many others, including the designers of the tanks on the display, attending. In addition to the A-20 and A-32, heavy KV, SMK and T-100, and light BT-7M and T-26 tanks were shown at the Kubinka proving ground in the Moscow region.

The A-32's performance was impressive. The tank easily surmounted all obstacles, including a ditch, an escarpment, a counter-escarpment, and a track bridge, and then crossed a river and climbed a 30-degree slope to finally knock down a thick pine-tree with the armoured bow of its hull, making the spectators applaud.

Following this demonstration, the opinion was voiced that thanks to the reserve of its thrust-to-weight ratio the A-32 might well be equipped with a thicker 45-mm armour, with some of its parts and components to be strengthened respectively.

An A-32 prototype, rear view.

KHARKOV TWINS

Meanwhile the experimental shop of Plant No 183 was assembling two tanks under the factory designation A-34. Apart from that, the A-32 trials with additional 6,380 kg of load were in full swing in October and November 1939. The vehicle's weight was increased to 24 tons by adding metal rails on its hull and turret. The test report signed by plant's Director Yu.Ye. Maksarev on 18 December 1939 reads: "The A-32 with additional load passed the tests satisfactorily."

The plant was rushing to assemble new tanks by 7 November, with all manufacturing powers devoted to this goal. However, certain technical difficulties emerged, mainly with power packs and power trains, which delayed assembly. All units and systems were fitted very carefully, with all threaded joints getting hot oil, and other moving parts being greased with purified lubricant. The protests of military representatives were ignored and only foreign bearings were used in gearboxes. Even outside surfaces of hulls and turrets were polished and specially treated.

The very intricate armour production technologies did not facilitate the rapid assembly of tanks either. For instance, the front armour of the hull was made of a one-piece armoured plate, hot-bent at a 10,000-ton press. The plate was heated, then bent, released, corrected, and dispatched for thermal processing again. Plates scorched from heating and cracked from bending, while their large size made finishing a very difficult job. The turret was welded from large bent armoured plates. All apertures in it, including the gun port, were cut out after bending which made mechanical processing extremely difficult.

Shortly after the tests, on 19 December 1939, the Defence Committee of the Council of People's Commissars adopted Resolution No 433ss on the adoption of tanks, armoured vehicles and artillery prime movers for service with the Red Army, and their mass production in 1940. The following was written in the document: "Proceeding from the results of the demonstrations and tests of new tanks, armoured vehicles and prime movers, built in compliance with Defence Committee's Resolutions No. 198ss dated 7 July 1938 and No. 118ss dated 15 May 1939, the Defence Committee under the Council of People's Commissars of the USSR resolved:

1. to adopt for service with the Red Army:

The T-32 fully-tracked tank powered by V-2 diesel engine, as developed by Plant No. 183, with the following design changes:

a) main armour plates' thickness increased to 45 mm;

b) crew vision improved;

c) the following armament installed:

1) the 76-mm F-32 gun with coaxial 7.62-mm machinegun;

2) a 7.62-mm radioman's machinegun;

3) a 7.62-mm fixed machinegun (editor's note: a spare MG carried inside the tank);

4) a 7.62-mm anti-aircraft machinegun, and designate the tank A-34."

An A-32 going off-road.

The first A-34 was rolled out in January 1940, and was followed by the second one in February. The vehicles were sent for field test at once. After running 250 km the engine of the first tank went out of order after only 25 hours of operation. It was replaced with a new one. By 26 February, the first vehicle had a mileage of 650 km, and the second had covered 350 km. It became clear that it would be impossible to complete the full test sequence of 2,000 km before the demonstration of the tanks to the government slated for March. The tanks would not have been allowed to be shown, unless the decision was taken to undertake a gruelling race from Kharkov to Moscow and thus cover the required mileage. M.I. Koshkin was appointed responsible for the organization of the race.

In the early morning of 5 March (or the night to 6 March according to other sources) a group of two A-34s and two Voroshilovets prime movers, one of which was refurbished for living purposes and the other stuffed full with all kinds of spares, headed for Moscow. With regard to secrecy, the team by-passed all large cities and avoided large roads. They were allowed to use bridges only if there were no ways to cross rivers on the ice, and only at night. The race schedule took into account all the trifles from time to sleep and move to the schedules of trains at railway lines to be crossed and even weather forecasts. The mean cruising speed was not to exceed 30 km/h.

The first troubles came shortly after they had passed Belgorod. The main clutch of one of the tanks went out of order when the vehicle was

going off-road in high snow. Some sources say this was due to the lack of experience of the driver, but this is unlikely, for the driving the tanks were entrusted to the best test drivers of the plant who had hundreds of miles in these particular vehicles. Yu.Ye. Maksarev gives a different point of view in his reminiscences. According to him, an AAD representative took control of the tank and started to make U-turns in snow at full speed, thus incapacitating the main clutch. M.I. Koshkin made the decision to continue the race with the remaining tank and call a repair team to rescue the broken vehicle.

In Serpukhov, the column was welcomed by A.A. Goreglyad, the Deputy People's Commissar for medium machine-building (the fact is that all tank manufacturing facilities were reassigned from the Defence Industry Commissariat to the Medium Machine Building Commissariat in 1939). The tank was sent to Moscow region's Plant No. 37 in Cherkizovo. During the few days before the other vehicle arrived lots of visitors came to see the new tank, including representatives of the Main Automobile and Armour Directorate, scholars of the Stalin engineering academy, top brass from the Red Army's General Staff, and others who were most interested to see the new tank. Koshkin fell seriously ill those days, for he had caught a cold during the race.

Overnight to 17 March both T-34s arrived in Ivanovskaya square in the Kremlin. Only the drivers of the production plant and Koshkin were admitted into the Kremlin territory, with operatives of the People's Commissariat for Interior Affairs (NKVD) seated in the tanks as gunners.

The second prototype of the A-32 tank, loaded to weigh 24 tonnes, during factory tests. Summer 1939.

Early in the morning a large group of Communist Party leaders and governmental officials approached the two tanks, including Stalin, Molotov, Kalinin, Beriya, Voroshilov and some others. AAD Chief D.G. Pavlov welcomed them, and then the floor was given to Koshkin. Despite the medicines he took he could not conceal his coughs, which annoyed Stalin and Beriya. After Koshkin finished his report and the country's top officials inspected the vehicles, the tanks moved away – one to the Spasskiye gate and the other to the Troitskiye gate. Right at the gates the two made steep U-turns and rushed across the square at a very high speed, striking sparkes from its paving stones. After several circles with sharp turns in all directions, the tanks stopped at their initial positions. The country's leader liked the vehicles and ordered that all possible assistance should be rendered to Plant No. 183 to eradicate the flaws in A-34 tanks to which Deputy People's Commissar of Defence G.I. Kulik and AAD Director D.G. Pavlov were persistently pointing. The latter was even bold enough to tell the "headman": "We will pay a very high price for building non-combatant vehicles."

A first prototype of the A-34 vehicle. Note bent front hull plate, which was not introduced in production vehicles.

PER ASPERA AD ASTRA

After the display in Kremlin, the tanks were dispatched to the proving ground in Kubinka, where their armour was subjected to trials with 45-mm rounds fired at them. After hits by two rounds from 100 m the glasses of periscopes and sights were broken, and the hinged armoured cap of the sight was torn off. In addition to that, the welded seams of the integrated sighting assemblies and at the bottom of the turret bustle cracked. As a result, the turret ring was distorted, and the turret stuck in place. A good thing was that the dummy crewman in the turret was intact, and the engine, started up prior to the trials, was still on. The decision was made to increase the turret bustle's bottom armour from 15 to 20 mm, and strengthen the fastening bolts of the rear hatch.

Running tests followed the shooting trials. The tanks had to climb 15-16 deg slopes, covered with 1.5 m of snow. The tests showed bad tractive resistance of the tracks. However, the vehicles proved superb in knocking down 700-mm thick pine-trees, and showed superior performance when exposed to water-tightness trials.

An experimental A-34 medium tank during field trials at Kubinka. March 1940.

The conclusion was eventually reached that A-34s met the requirements specified, and was superior to all in-service tanks of the Red Army. However, the A-34 tank was not put into series until the shortcomings and flaws revealed during the tests were eradicated.

On 31 March 1940 the first experimental vehicle of the renewed A-34 was brought for inspection by top military and political officials, with Defence Commissar Voroshilov, his deputy Kulik, chief of AAD Pavlov, Commissar for medium machine-building I.A. Likhachev, his deputy Goreglyad and chief designer Koshkin attending. As a result Protocol No. 848 was signed authorising T-34 (A-34) mass production at Plant No. 183 and the Stalingrad Tractor Works (STZ). Remarks were made, however, that the turret should be made more spacious to ensure more comfort for the crew. All modifications of the turret were to be achieved without changing the slant angles of its armoured plates or increasing the turret ring diameter. The radio was to be moved from the turret into the hull. The official tank test commission was tasked to draft and approve new blueprints of the T-34 within five days for its mass production to start in 1940.

The final stage of the official trials was the return race of the tanks in April 1940. Upon arrival in Kharkov after covering 3,000 km, certain defects were discovered when the tanks were disassembled: brakes and ferrodo on the

disks of main clutches were slightly burnt, small cracks were noticeable in the fans, and there were lots of chips and splits of gear teeth in the gearboxes. The design bureau thought about ways to improve the situation, but it was clear to all that a production A-34 would not be able to meet its 3,000 km guaranteed mileage without breakdowns, even after improvements had been made.

Meanwhile, the plant's leadership had approved the production plan for 1940, with 150 A-34s envisaged to be released. The plan was soon subjected to significant corrections, however: on 5 June 1940 the Council of USSR People's Commissars and the Central Committee of the Communist Party adopted a resolution on the production of T-34 tanks in 1940, which read:

"Taking account of the special importance attributed to the need to equip the Red Army with T-34 tanks, the Council of People's Commissars and the Central Committee of the Communist Party herby resolve:

1. To empower People's Commissioner for Medium Machine-Building Comrade Likhachev:

a) to supervise the production of 600 T-34 tanks in 1940, of which

500 pcs. to be built by Komintern Plant No 183, and

100 pcs. to be built by the Stalingrad tractor works;

The second prototype of the A-34 tank during fire-extinguishing tests. Spring 1940. The driver's "raised hood" is clearly seen, which was available for this vehicle only.

b) to ensure supplies of engines in fulfilment of the 1940 program of T-34 tank production, for which V-2 diesel production at Plant No. 75 should be enhanced, with 2,000 engines built before end of 1940.

The heads of subcontracting enterprises under the T-34 program should be instructed that they bear personal responsibility for the timely and quality production and supplies of all required spares and units."

Despite these fearsome warnings the plan was never put into action in full; moreover, clouds came over the T-34 program in summer 1940. The fact was that two Pz.III tanks were brought to Kubinka, purchased from Germany after the non-aggression pact was signed between the countries. The comparative tests of German tanks and T-34s were disappointing for the Soviet combat vehicle.

The T-34 was superior to its German rival in armour and armament, but was very much inferior in other ways. The Pz. III had a three-man turret, quite comfortable for the crewmembers. The commander's cupola was convenient and ensured superb vision, and all crewmen had interphone arrangements. Unlike that, a T-34 turret could hardly accommodate two crewmen, one of them dual-tasked as both gunner and tank commander, and in some cases even as commander of a larger formation. Interphone communications were available only for the commander and driver.

The German tank was smoother on the move, and turned out to make far less noise than the Russian counterpart – travelling at full speed

Pz. III was heard from 150-200 meters, while the noise of the T-34 was clearly detectable from as far as 450 m.

The German tank's speed superiority was also a severe blow to the Soviet military: during trials on the unpaved road from Kubinka to Repishche, the Pz III attained a speed of 69.7 km/h, while the T-34's best was only 48.2 km/h. The BT-7, said to be the fastest and therefore chosen for comparison, could accelerate only to 68.1 km/h!

The comparative test report praised the better suspension of the German tank, better quality of its optics, more convenient stowing arrangements and the location of the radio, as well as the more reliable engine and transmission.

The results of the trials were like a bomb blast. The Main Automobile and Armour Directorate (the successor of the Automobile and Armour Directorate of the Red Army since July 1940) submitted the test report to Marshal Kulik, who approved it and suspended the production and acceptance of T-34s until all the shortcomings were eradicated. The leadership of Plant No. 183 disagreed with the customer and brought its complaints to the people's commissariat, where it offered to continue the production of the T-34 version in renewed configuration with the guaranteed mileage reduced to 1,000 km. People's Commissar of Medium Machine-Building V.A. Malyshev, who had succeeded Likhachev in position, and chief of the 8th Main Directorate of the People's Commissariat of Medium Machine-Building Goreglyad, together with Plant No. 183 Director Maksarev and head of the research and development committee under the MAAD I.A. Lebedev turned to Klement Voroshilov, who, like Malyshev, was a deputy chairman of the Council of People's Commissars of the USSR. Voroshilov studied the report of the 3,000 km race of the tank, its tests at the former Mannerheim Line, listened carefully to Lebedev, who spoke for the continuation of the T-34 production, and resolved: "The plant shall continue assembling new vehicles, and supplying them to the army with 1,000-km guaranteed mileage. At the same time, the plant shall start the development of a new vehicle, to be designated the T-34M, that alongside with armour improvements should have five-speed gearbox added."

Koshkin, who had had pneumonia since March, felt very bad by that time. Despite the removal of the affected lung he passed away on 26 September 1940, and Morozov succeeded him as the chief designer of the tank design bureau.

The latter led the development of two variants of upgraded T-34s. In the first prototype, designated A-41, an attempt was made to remedy most of the disadvantages without making a new hull and replacing the power pack. The vehicle got a new three-seat turret with a ring diameter of 1,700 mm (against 1,420 mm on the original T-34) and the new gun, F-34, built by Plant No. 92. However, the project was never implemented.

The second variant was designated A-43, but is renowned as T-34M. It was longer and higher than the T-34, with the ground clearance increased by 50 mm. A new engine, the V-5 devel-

oping 600 hp, was designed to propel the tank. The old transmission was retained, but a demultiplier was introduced in addition to the previously used four-speed gearbox. As a result, the A-43 had eight forward and two reverse gears. The tank's Christie-type suspension, inherited from the BT, was replaced by torsion bars.

The turret of the A-43, like that of the A-41, featured a commander's cupola and two access hatches. The radio was moved into the hull, which allowed expanding main armament stowage from 77 to 100 rounds, while the machinegun's ammunition load was increased from 46 to 72 magazines.

The resulting vehicle weighed 987 kg less than the original T-34, but its ground pressure increased thanks to the track made 100-mm narrower.

In addition to the development of the new A-43, Plant No. 183 never stopped assembling T-34s, though not quite successfully. For instance, in June 1940 only four of the planned ten vehicles were built. The delays were due to the fact that welders were engaged in the production of BT-7M tanks and plant Director Maksarev, despite the repeated requests of the military, was refusing to let them be involved in T-34 assembly until late in June. As a result, of 16 sets of subassemblies for turrets and hulls shipped by the Mariupol plant, only five hulls were ready in June.

Subcontractors were not in the least effective in supplying subassemblies for T-34s either. The worst case was with the Stalingrad Tractor Works

One of the first production T-34s. The vehicle does not have the protective armoured collar around the driver's hatch cover. 1940.

(STZ) that did not make a single part from 90 items long list by 1 July 1940. As of 25 June, only 200 of the 11,100 track links planned were delivered to Kharkov from Stalingrad. The Ilyich metallurgic plant in Mariupol supplied armoured parts that needed additional processing, for they did not match geometrically. Despite the simplified production technologies, with the front armour of the hull now assembled of the top and bottom plates and a nose piece, the process was still quite troublesome and labour consuming, unlike that of the BT-7M tank whose production did not end until July 1940.

Plant No. 75 did its best to ensure V-2 engine's trouble-free operation for 150 hours on the bench. There were quite a few problems with the power pack! To ensure correct and generalised fuel injection and supply, special benches were built to test the whole set of 12 injectors with all fuel pumps and pipelines. Extramural students were called to duty to manually adjust valves, injectors and needles. Notably girls were very good at it, because their narrow fingers suited the job best. Lots of troubles were encountered with injector apertures. 0.3 mm in diameter drills were used at fast rotary speeds to make six holes in the injectors. These, really jewellers' tools, were kept in matchboxes. One such box was enough for only one shift.

The armament of the new tank was yet another issue demanding thorough consideration. Under Resolution No. 443 dated 19 December 1939, the T-34 was to be armed with a 76-mm F-32 gun developed by Plant No. 92's special design bureau led by V.G. Grabin. The Defence Committee adopted the gun for service by its Resolution No. 45 dated 25 January 1940, with the Kirov plant tasked to start its mass-production in 1940 instead of the L-11 gun of the same calibre that was decommissioned in 1939. The plant was assigned to make an initial batch of 30 F-32 guns in the first half of 1940, and start their mass-production on August 1. However, the Kirov plant disliked the "alien" weapon intensely as it was promoting its own L-11 design. The plant's leadership even won V.A. Malyshev's support in this respect. However, it did not help: comparative tests of both guns in May 1940 proved the F-32 to be much superior to the L-11. Under the plans corrected in August 1940 the Kirov plant was to make 130 F-32s by the year-end, but managed to assemble only 50, installable into heavy KV tanks in January 1941.

In summary, the L-11 turned out to be the only weapon available to be installed in T-34s in 1940. Although these guns were no longer in production and were delivered to Kharkov from artillery depots, rather than from manufacturing plants, the lack of them was still felt keenly. The problem was that the same gun was mounted on the heavy KV tanks and a number of experimental armoured vehicles. As a result, a total of 453 T-34s were rolled out with this gun as the main armament.

Starting in summer 1940, the design bureau of Plant No. 92 began developing a 76-mm F-34 weapon to arm A-41 and A-43 prototypes. A mock-up of the gun was brought to Kharkov from Gorky where it was under development at the request of Plant No. 183's Director Maksarev. The

A production T-34 mod 1940 armed with 76-mm L-11 gun.

mock-up differed from the combat version only with the absence of rifling in its bore. Meanwhile the factory tests of the F-34 ended, and the weapon was brought to the attention of the acceptance commission of the Defence Committee on 21 October. It was installed in a BT-7 A though, rather than in the A-41. No decisions were made by the commission, but an opinion was universally supported that the F-34 would suit production T-34 tanks without necessitating an increase of its turret ring diameter. Mention should be made that, for certain production reasons, the gun length was to be shortened to 40 calibres. Despite such a "modernisation", the F-34 was still much more powerful than either the F-32 or L-11, which had lengths of 30.5 calibres.

In early December 1940 the Defence Committee resolved to put the F-34 into mass production, though no decision was yet made that it should be adopted for military service. Plant No. 92 used for the first time the so-called "fast method" for the development of the F-34. Grabin noted in his reminiscences that this method allowed assembly of such weapons to start only 13 days after the decision was made to put them

into mass production. In February 1941 Plant No. 92 shipped 82 F-34s to Kharkov, and as early as March reached the planned production rates. Notably, the decision to commission the gun for service was not adopted until July 1941.

But back to 1940. In July that year only one tank was assembled at the experimental workshop of Plant No. 183, instead of the 20 planned, with another two following in August. Only in September did the plant manage to hand over 37 tanks to the military. Due to the lack of L-11 guns, the military accepted only one vehicle in October, with another 55 assembled tanks standing without armament. As early as November 1940, Plant No 183 not only built 35 tanks, but managed to dispatch sets of hulls, turrets, guns and sights ready for assembly of 12 T-34s at the Stalingrad Tractor Works.

Meanwhile the first three production T-34 tanks were subjected to intensive trials at the Kubinka proving ground in November and December in compliance with the directive issued by the deputy defence commissar on 25 October 1940. They also performed a gruelling 38-day trip en route Kharkov-Moscow-Smolensk-

A production T-34 tank. The driver's hatch cover is equipped with the protective collar, bridging the gap between the cover and the hull front plate. Armoured strips were added around the hatch cover to prevent spall from getting inside the hatch when the tank was exposed to machinegun fire.

A wooden mock-up of the T-43 tank.

Gomel-Kiev-Poltava-Kharkov. In addition, firing tests were undertaken at the halt and on the move in which 249 main gun and 1,423 machinegun rounds were fired. The specialists of the proving ground found so many flaws and shortcomings in the design of the new vehicles that they even doubted if T-34 were combat worthy at all. The issue was raised once again to stop production of such tanks, more so that the leaders at the MAAD and the Defence Commissariat were dead certain that the light T-50 tanks should be the most numerous in service with the Red Army.

MAAD's Chief Ya.N. Fedorenko and G.I. Kulik, the head of the Main Artillery Directorate, were supported by D.G. Pavlov, the Commander of the Western Special Military District, in their initiative to stop the production of T-34s and resume that of BT-7Ms until the development of the T-34M was completed. However, their proposal was declined.

AT THE THRESHOLD OF WAR

Speaking of the T-34M (A-43), the Defence Committee under the Council of People's Commissars of the USSR approved the new design in January 1941, and as early as March this year the assembly of the first two prototypes started. Meanwhile, subcontractors were preparing for the production of spare parts, accessories and units for the new vehicle.

The 45-mm thick drop-forged turret was developed by the Mariupol metallurgic plant under V.S. Nitsenko. In May 1941 the plant made the first five turrets of the kind and prepared its facilities for mass production (about 50 semi-fin-

ished turrets were taken from Mariupol during the evacuation in the autumn 1941). At about the same time, die-cast turrets with 52-mm thick walls started to be produced at the plant.

A reflection of all the hardships, disagreements and controversies, the resolution of the Council of People's Commissars of the USSR was issued on 5 May 1941 concerning the production of T-34s in 1941, which said:

"1. The People's Commissariat of Medium Machine-Building shall ensure the production in 1941 as follows:

	Plant No. 183	STZ
Total in 1941	1,800	1,000
Before1 May	525	130
May	140	60
June	150	80
July	160	100
August	175	110
September	175	110
October	150	130
November	160	130
December	165	150

a) 2,800 T-34 tanks, including 1,800 at Plant No. 183 and 1,000 at STZ, for which the following supply schedule shall apply:

2. Authorise People's Commissar of Medium Machine-Building Comrade Malyshev and Plnat

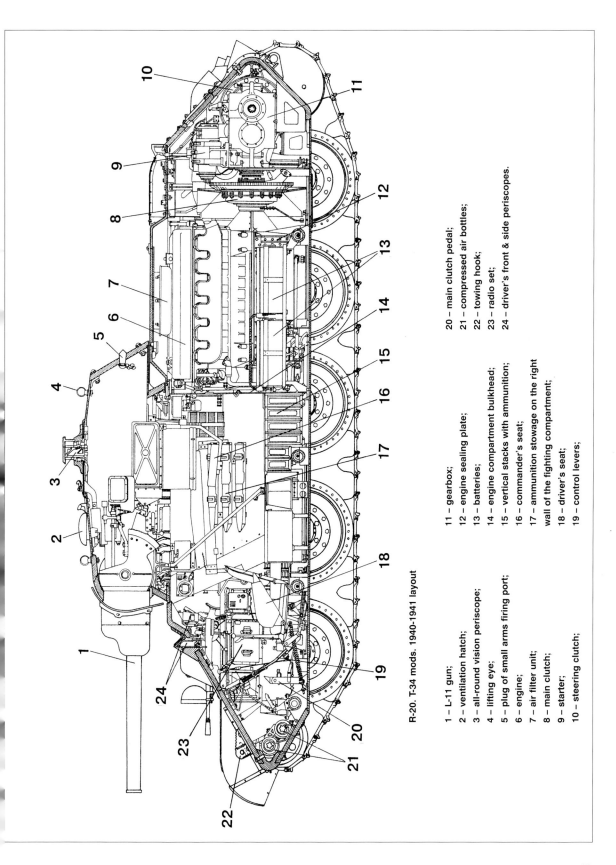

R-20. T-34 mods. 1940-1941 layout

1 – L-11 gun;
2 – ventilation hatch;
3 – all-round vision periscope;
4 – lifting eye;
5 – plug of small arms firing port;
6 – engine;
7 – air filter unit;
8 – main clutch;
9 – starter;
10 – steering clutch;

11 – gearbox;
12 – engine sealing plate;
13 – batteries;
14 – engine compartment bulkhead;
15 – vertical stacks with ammunition;
16 – commander's seat;
17 – ammunition stowage on the right
wall of the fighting compartment;
18 – driver's seat;
19 – control levers;

20 – main clutch pedal;
21 – compressed air bottles;
22 – towing hook;
23 – radio set;
24 – driver's front & side periscopes.

A T-34 with 76-mm F-34 gun during tests at the Gorokhovets proving ground. November 1940.

No. 183 Director Comrade Maksarev to ensure that the following improvements are made in the T-34 design:

a) turret armour and hull front armour increased to 60 mm;

b) torsion-bar suspension to be applied for the running gear;

c) turret ring to be expanded to at least 1,600 mm, with a commander's cupola added for all-round vision;

d) tank hull sides to be vertical, with side armour thickness to be as effective as 40-mm armour sloped at 45 deg.

3. The full combat weight of the improved T-34 to be set at 27.5 tonnes.

4. Authorise People's Commissar of Medium Machine-Building Comrade Malyshev and Plant No. 183 Director Comrade Maksarev to ensure the production of 500 improved T-34s in 1941 within the framework of the program, to be launched with this resolution."

References in this document were made to both the T-34 and the T-34M, because everything was ready to put the latter into series as well. By 17 April Kharkov had made three armoured hulls, with torsion bars, road wheels and other running gear elements having come to the plant later that month. However, the V-5 engine, intended to pro-

pel this tank, had not been finished either by 1 May or by the outset of the war.

The T-34 production program was quite tough, demanding all the powers of the plant to be concentrated on it. Non-standard, break-through solutions were needed, including the introduction of automatic welding of hulls and turrets. Such a method was first tested in Kharkov in May 1941. Plant Director Maksarev described this process in his reminiscences, an extract from which is hereunder:

"Calculations showed that we don't have enough welders, transformers and assembly equipment to produce hulls and turrets. As a follow-up of consultations with the Central Committee of the Communist Party and the respective People's Commissariat, a prominent scientist from Kiev, Yevgeny Oskarovich Paton, was sent to assist. Attending the 12th conference of the Ukrainian communist party, I heard a lot about this outstanding and really gifted scientist, and even saw the experimental bridge, erected under the plans set forth in his graduation thesis at the Vladimir hill. However, here the work had nothing to do with bridging and framework constructions. When I first met Paton at the doors of the director's office, he was very angry. I found out what the reason for his anger was, and talked him into returning to my office, where I also called all executives and workshop masters. I was struck by the stubbornness of the welders, quality managers, military representatives and technologists, who refused point blank to adopt "Paton weld method" (automatic submerged arch welding).

However, at the end of the heated debate I insisted that this state-of-the-art method should be adopted! But an experiment should first be conducted. First, we had to build a Glagol radial machine that would move on rails along the welding mechanism to be used to weld two 45-mm thick armour plates at 90 deg. The institute agreed to make the welding head and inform us how many ST-32 weld transformers we would have to prepare. Military representative Comrade Zukher, who was the senior military representative concerned with all armoured constructions, said he would not accept the weld made in such a manner without shooting trials to verify the strength of the seam.

After some time, Chief Mechanic Kutsykovich and Designer Voloshin reported that the Glagol was ready for tests. We called for Paton in Kiev and set the time of the test. The free shifts of welders, certified to weld armour, and amour pro-duction technologists, quality management personnel, designers, S.N. Makhonin and I came to witness the process. The armour plates, with lengths equal to those of the nose plate of the T-34 tank, were put in position and fixed with screws so that there was an angled hollow between them.

The operator wore no glasses, which was a great surprise for us. He added some welding flux into the hollow, straightened it, took the welding head and the electrode wire, and turned on the transformer. We heard hissing and cracking, and the flux began to distort. The operator was pushing the machine along the rails, and we could see the wire unwinding from the roll and submerging into the flux, which continued boiling behind it. Our welders put on dark glasses. Chief of the armoured hulls department Comrade Savostin was pressing me to put on dark glasses used in metallurgic industry to watch the boiling steel, and all were hissing into my ears to avoid watching the welding process unprotected. But I trusted the operator who wore no glasses. Finally, the seam was ready, which took five or six times less than it normally took to make such a weld manually. The operator brushed the residual flux into the bucket, and

A T-34 mod. 1941 tank. Note that the port to accommodate the all-round periscope in the turret roof hatch cover has been plugged.

we noticed the seam, which looked like a bubbled snake stuck between the plates. The welding experts, especially quality managers and military representatives, were quite dissatisfied, and Comrade Savostin even said that as long as he was responsible for hull welding, he would not let such seams pass!

However, Paton and the operator were calm. The operator hit the seam with the tool normally used to dispose of the oxide scale and we were surprised at seeing the real seam – a very plain, glittering line that filled the space between the two plates entirely. Everybody was stunned.

They welded another two plates, and then welded the resultant construction with the first joint, and Comrade Zukher took it away to his firing range to test by shooting. He told me by phone later that he had broken the armour into pieces, but failed to break the seams.

This was a decisive victory for the scientist and his institute!

We agreed to start assembling machines for the welding of the tank nose, and assigned technologists to study the possibilities of applying Paton welding, as we decided to call it for short, for welding other parts of the hull. This method allowed us to reduce the requirement for welders five or even six times. At that time we were far from thinking of a welding conveyor, because we were still quite all right, welding hulls manually."

In the first half of 1941 the military accepted 816 T-34s from Plant No. 183 and 294 from STZ, which means that a total of 1,225 tanks had been available for army service by 1 July 1941. In June 58 of them were still at the production plants, pending dispatch for service.

DIFFICULT 1941

On 25 June 1941 the Council of People's Commissars of the USSR and the Central Committee of the Communist Party issued a joint resolution to increase the production of KV, T-34 and T-50 tanks, artillery prime movers and tank diesel engines in the third and fourth quarters of 1941. The document formulated a task to create a full-scale tank-building industry. Plant No. 183 and STZ were authorised to stop commercial production and mobilize capabilities in order to be ready to assist other plants to produce T-34s. On 1 July 1941 another resolution was issued by the State Defence Committee under No. 1ss, authorising the Krasnoye Sormovo plant in Gorky (also known as Plant No. 112 of the People's Commissariat of Shipbuilding Industry) to join the production of T-34 tanks. The Kharkov tractor works was assigned the mission to produce gearboxes, steering clutches, power trains, drive sprockets and road wheels for the tank.

Meanwhile Plant No. 183 was increasing output. People were working in two shifts of 11 hours each, and did not leave workshops even during the bombings in the city. As a result, 225 tanks were

The cast turret of a T-34 mod. 1942. The gun dismounting hatch cover in the turret rear was attached with six bolts.

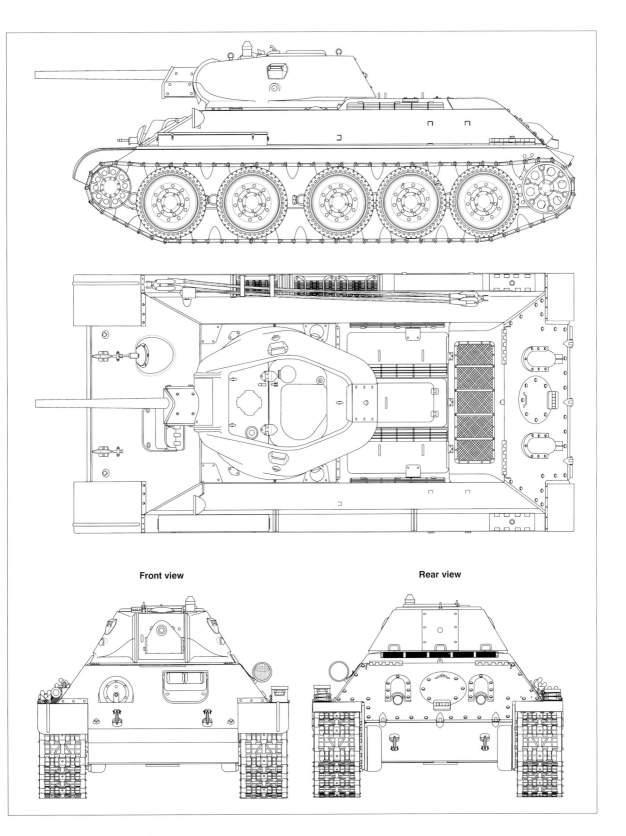

Front view

Rear view

A T-34 mod. 1942, built by Plant No. 183

A T-34 assembled at Plant No. 183 in Nizhny Tagil in winter/spring 1942.

rolled out of the plant's gate in July, 250 in August and 250 in September. The last 30 were assembled at the plant in September just before the evacuation. Pursuant to Resolution No. 667 of the State Defence Committee dated 12 September 1941, Maksarev issued an order to immediately evacuate the plant into the depths of USSR territory. The first trainload left Kharkov on 19 September heading for Nizhny Tagil in the Urals, to be re-established around the Ural railroad car factory. The Ordzhonikidze engineering plant arrived at the same facilities from Moscow, as well as the Krasny Proletariy, Stankolit and some other plants. All these were merged into the Ural Tank Plant No. 183 which assembled its first 25 tanks from the parts brought from Kharkov as early as late December.

In autumn 1941 STZ remained the only large manufacturer of the T-34. The production of as many parts and units as possible was launched in Stalingrad. Armour came from Krasny Oktyabr and was welded into hulls at the Stalingrad shipyard (Plant No. 264), and the guns were supplied by Barrikady. In other words, almost the entire production cycle of subassemblies and tanks proper was launched in Stalingrad, and the output was naturally growing. Whereas in June and July 86 and 93 tanks were respectively accepted by the military from Stalingrad, in August the number grew to 155! The greatest output of tanks was reached by the plant in September, when the record of 165 combat vehicles was attained. In

October, though, only 124 tanks were handed over, which was because there were no more shipments of hulls and turrets from the evacuated Plant No. 183.

The production of V-2 diesels was also very slow. In mid-1941 the only manufacturer of such engines was Plant No. 75 in Kharkov, followed by the Kharkov tractor works, authorised to be engaged in engine production pursuant to the resolution issued in the first days of the war. However, the contingency at the front made the leadership alter the plans. Engine production moved from Kharkov to STZ, where diesels started to come out in November 1941. Plant No. 75 was evacuated to the Ural Mountains, which meant that no V-2 engines were produced for some time. To somehow reduce the impact, M-17 carburettor motors were installed in some tanks.

Such an opportunity was raised as an issue for discussion by Plant No. 183 as far back as June 1941. The work was stepped up following the issuance of the resolution by the Council of People's Commissars on 16 September 1941, regulating the introduction of the M-17 engine into the T-34. Only five days after the resolution was passed, all documentation was handed over to STZ and Plant No. 112.

The Stalingrad Tractor Works equipped 209 of its tanks with M-17 engines in 1941, and another 364 in the period from January to March 1942. Mention should be made that in 95 of the tanks

T-34 crew camouflaging their tank in a trench, 1942. The vehicle was apparently built by STZ in late 1941, judging from some of the elements it is made of.

A T-34 assembled at STZ in late 1941 featuring all-metal road wheels and non-rubber-tyred wheels.

Supposedly, the only existing T-34 built at Plant No. 183 in Kharkov in 1941. The vehicle is kept among the exhibits of the Kubinka Armour History Museum. 2002.

A just completed T-34 leaving the workshop of Plant No. 112 Krasnoye Sormovo. Spring 1942.

assembled in March, M-17s were replaced with V-2s in April.

The T-34 production program of the Krasnoye Sormovo plant envisaged 700-750 tanks to be made in 1941 but only 173 were assembled by the year-end, of which 156 were powered by M-17 engines. Another 540 T-34 with carburettor engines were rolled out from the plant's workshops in 1942.

Plant No. 75 was redeployed in Chelyabinsk, where it merged with the Chelyabinsk-based Kirov plant. In November 1941 the first 18 diesels were assembled there from the parts brought from Kharkov, and as early as December that year the plant launched full-scale mass-production of engines from its own parts, with 155 power packs readied by the end of the year. In January 1942 a total of 240 diesels were assembled, and by March 1942 the production rate had reached 10 engines per day. However, even such high rates were no match for the requirements of the tank builders.

With this in mind, the Council of People's Commissars resolved to begin the production of diesels at another two plants. The engine-building department of the Leningrad Kirov plant was evacuated to Sverdlovsk-based Ural Turbine Works (renamed Plant No. 76 on 13 December), where the first engine was assembled on 12 October 1941.

The cast turret from Pant No. 112 without a gun-dismounting hatch in the rear.

Yet another plant was opened in Altai. On 13 October 1941 the State Defence Committee agreed to start the construction of two plants in Barnaul: one to produce light T-50 tanks, and the other to build 6-cylinder V-4 engine for the tank. In the late January 1942, the two were re-established as one named Plant No. 77, and as early as 17 September 1942 the new factory was authorised to produce V-2 diesels. Engine production

A T-34 tank built at Krasnoye Sormovo, retired to serve as an exhibit of the Central Museum of the Great Patriotic War in Moscow. 2005.

The all-welded
turret of the
Stalingrad plant:
the detachable
rear plate is proof
of that. Its large
turret hatch was
far from a brilliant
design solution,
but its cover was
a good protection
for crewmembers
when they got
half-out of the
hatch to observe
the battlefield.
Kalinin Front,
3rd Guards Tank
Brigade, spring
1942.

was launched there based on the tools and machinery of the evacuated Kharkov Tractor Works and the Moscow ZIS plant.

THE CONTRIBUTION OF PLANTS

In summary, three plants were involved in T-34 production in late 1941 and the first half of 1942 – Plant No. 183, redeployed in Nizhny Tagil, STZ, and Plant No. 112 Krasnoye Sormovo. Plant No. 183 was the prime contractor, as also was its Section 520 design bureau (GKB-54 according to other sources) as far as tank design was concerned. All alterations and amendments in the T-34 design were supposed to be approved there, but de-facto the situation was quite different: the requirements specified remained intact, while the tanks of different manufacturers sometimes differed greatly.

For instance, on 25 October 1941 Plant No. 112 started making experimental hulls, with the edges of their armour plates not subjected to mechanical processing after gas cutting, and interlocked joints of the front armour plate with the sides and the sponson bottoms.

There was a hatch in the back of the turret with a detachable armoured cover fixed by six bolts in the original design diagram of the tank. The hatch was intended for field-dismantling of a damaged gun. Metallurgists of the Krasnoye Sormovo plant cast the turret in one piece and then cut out the hatch in its back. But combat engagements showed that the detachable hatch cover vibrated too much when the machinegun was fired, which normally caused breakdown of fixtures and detaching of the cover. Attempts were repeatedly made to get rid of the hatch in the design, but in vain, mostly because of counter-arguments of the military, who wanted to retain the gun-removal capability in the field. To solve the riddle, chief of the plant's armament department A.S. Okunev suggested that the turret bustle could be raised with the help of two tank jacks, in which case the gun, disconnected from the trunnions, would be freely removable through the space that opened between the turret ring and the hull roof. During the tests, a stopper was welded onto the hull roof in front of the turret to prevent turret slide during jacking. Turrets without rear hatches started to be produced at Plant No. 112

on 1 March 1941. Military Representative A.A. Afanasiev suggested in his turn that instead of the stopper an armoured collar should be welded across the hull width, which would simultaneously prevent the turret from sliding and protect the gap at the turret neck from bullets, spalls and fragments. Later on, this collar and the absence of the hatch in the turret rear were the distinctive characteristics of T-34s built at Krasnoye Sormovo.

Tank-builders were forced to demonstrate miraculous creativity in their work, while many of their subcontractors were gone. For instance, when air bottles from Dnepropetrovsk for engine start-up in cold weather were no longer available, Krasnoye Sormovo started using cases from artillery rounds in their roles, sorted out for mechanical processing failures!

STZ followed suit to apply whatever it had at hand: many welded and forged parts of the tank were replaced with cast ones, thanks to the fact that the plant's casting workshops were reputed the second largest in the world at that time. Starting in August 1941, the plant was running short of rubber and had to introduce cast road wheels

with internal shock-absorbing into its T-34 tanks, first released on 29 October. The resultant peculiarity of the Stalingrad-made tanks was the absence of rubber tyres on all road wheels. Also, a new-design track was developed featuring a flattened tread, which helped reduce the noise made by the moving tank. Rubber tyres were also later removed from the drive sprockets and idlers.

Yet another feature of the tanks built in Stalingrad was the simplified hull and turret production technology, introduced by Plant No. 264 to keep up with Krasnoye Sormovo. Armoured parts were interconnected by pins. Traditional joints were retained only where the top hull plate connected with the roof plate, and the bottom plate with the nose and rear plates. Thanks to the reduced mechanical processing requirements, the hull assembly time was reduced from nine to two days. As for the turret, it was welded of untreated armour plates and then subjected to hardening. As a result, the need fell to adjust turret elements after hardening, while its installation onto the tank also became easier.

A knocked-out T-34 built by STZ in spring/summer 1942. This was the final version of the tank as assembled in Stalingrad, which is proved by many of features: the mantlet is the simplified design of the Barrikady plant; all hull plates are interconnected by interlocked joints; the front bottom of the turret is a sloped plate.

The Stalingrad Tractor Works built and repaired tanks until the front line came close to the workshops. The situation report from Workshop 5 of the plant for the period from 23 August to 12 September 1942 casts light on the real conditions in which people had to work:

"Since fascists have approached the plant, with resultant bombings and shootouts, Workshop 5 has managed to perform the work as follows: released 68 new tanks and repaired 23 tanks. We also helped the Red Army by dispatching qualified specialists to assist repair teams, as well as by providing them with spares, tools and equipment.

For the period, six high-explosive bombs, about 154 incendiary bombs and one artillery round hit the building. A lubricant store has burnt down to the ground, and the roof is broken in two places."

On 5 October 1942 the plant was closed and its employees evacuated.

This left Plant No. 183 the main manufacturer of T-34s in 1942, but it could not adopt the planned production rates after evacuation for some time. As a result, the plans of the first three months were never accomplished. The later increase in the tank output was based, on the one hand, on the clear and rational organization of the production flow, and on the reduction of labour-consumption on the other. A detailed reconsideration of the tank design was undertaken, which brought about simplified production of 770 items and total abolishment of 5,641 items of the tank. Another 206 items, previously shipped by subcontractors, were also recognized unnecessary. In this light, the mechanical assembling time reduced from 260 to 80 standard hours.

The running gear of the tank was subjected to a total reconsideration. For instance, the road wheels were cast and without rubber tyres, like those in Stalingrad. Starting in January 1942, three or four such wheels were installable on tanks on each side. Rubber tyres were also removed from the idler and the drive sprocket, and the latter was now cast with no rollers.

The oil radiator of the lubricating system was removed, while the oil tank capacity was increased to 50 litres. The fuel system's rotary gear pump was replaced by a rotary lobular pump. The insufficient supplies of electronic

A T-34 assembled by STZ, knocked out in combat near the Don River. July 1942. The vehicle is apparently of a later series, as its non-detachable rear turret wall is welded.

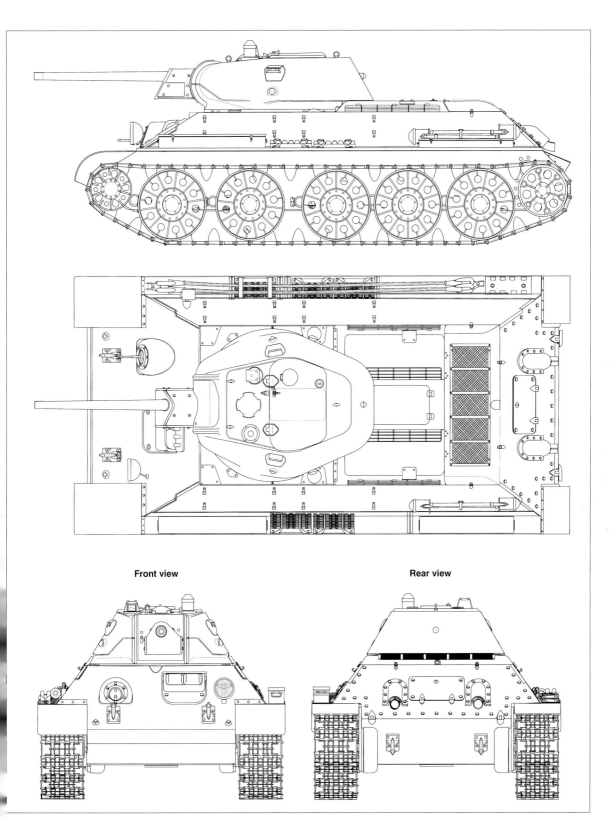

Front view

Rear view

A T-34 rolled out from STZ in summer 1942.

A T-34 tank of the Polish tank regiment during the parade on the occasion of the swearing in of the 1st Kosciuszko Polish Infantry Division. July 1943. The vehicle originates from Krasnoye Sormovo and has additional armour protection on the hull front – an appliqué armour plate.

equipment made the installation of some gauges and measuring systems, headlights, taillights, electric fan, horn and tank interphones impossible until the spring 1942.

It should be stressed that in some cases the design alterations undertaken to simplify construction and reduce the production time were unreasonable. Some of them later affected the performance of the T-34 on the battlefield.

Some sources say that T-34s were provided with front hull armour 60-mm thick since 1942. However, this is not quite right. It is true that the State Defence Committee meeting on 25 October1941 issued Resolution No. 1062 envisaging that T-34s should have 60-mm armour on the hull front starting from 15 February 1942. This resolution was most likely adopted in view of the fact that Germans were increasing the number in the service of 50-mm Pak 38 antitank guns with barrel lengths of 60 calibres. Fired from such guns, armour-piercing and armour-piercing discarding sabot rounds were quite effective in killing T-34s through their front armour at ranges up to 1,000 m. Moreover, Pz III tanks, armed with L/42 guns, fired 50-mm APDS rounds, which were equally lethal to Soviet T-34s at 500 m.

Because the metallurgic plants could not quickly satisfy the needs for 60-mm armoured plates, tank manufacturers were told to reinforce the fronts of hulls and turrets with 10-15-mm plates, as used by Plant No. 264 in the production of hulls for T-60 tanks. However, the State Defence Committee recalled its decision on 23 February 1942, partly because of the difficulties to make 60-mm thick plates, and partly because the Germans did not use APDS rounds often. Nevertheless, tanks with such reinforcements on hulls and turrets were built at STZ and Plant No 112 until early March 1942, when the stocks of their plates were exhausted. Krasnoye Sormovo cast eight tank turrets with 75-mm thick armour, and additionally made 68 T-34s with skirts on hulls and turrets in the autumn 1942. The skirts were intended to protect the tanks from shaped-charge attacks, but this assumption had never been put to trial, as almost all the vehicles were destroyed in their first battle by German 75-mm antitank rounds. Skirts were no longer applied to the tanks, because Germans did not often resort to shaped-charge munitions.

The increase in the production of T-34s in 1942 was to a large extent a result of the introduction of the automatic submerged arc welding method, developed by Academician Ye.O. Paton, first at Plant No. 183 and later at all other plants. It was not a coincidence that Plant No. 183 was the leader in this, for the Institute of Electric Welding under the Academy of Sciences of the Ukrainian Soviet Socialist Republic was also evacuated to Nizhny Tagil's Ural Tank Plant.

In January 1942 an experimental hull was made, with one side welded manually and the other side and the nose by submerged arc welding. The hull was taken to a firing range for strength tests. It was shot at from short ranges, when almost all the kinetic energy of rounds was absorbed by the armoured plate. Paton then wrote in his reminiscences: "The tank was subjected to a severe test by shooting from short ranges with armour-piercing and high-explosive rounds. The first hit on the side welded manually resulted in the cracking of the seam. The hull was then turned with the other side forward. The automatically welded seam withstood seven direct hits! Moreover, it was stronger than the armour itself. The seam in the nose proved equally effective. This was the full and entire victory of fast automatic welding."

A welding conveyor line was introduced at the plant. Several car bogies were rolled into the workshop, with patterns cut in them to match tank hull sides. A construction of beams was erected above the bogies so that the welding heads could travel along and across the beams. Then the bogies were connected and the conveyor line was ready for operation. Lateral seams were welded at the first station, longitudinal at the second. Then the hull was put on one side, and then on the other. The bottom plate was welded at the final station. Some of the welds were made manually, where it was impossible to apply automatic welding. Thanks to the conveyor hull production time was reduced five times. By the end of 1942, Plant No. 183 alone had six such conveyor lines, and in late 1943 their total number at all tank building plants reached 15, and 30 a year after.

Welding issues settled, cast turret production was still an issue, because ground dies were used. Such technology required significant work for the cutting and removal of dead-heads and drop gates in the seams between mould blocks. Plant's Chief Metallurgist P.P. Malyarov and head of the steel-casting foundry I.I. Atopov suggested that mechanical moulding should be applied. However, a totally different

A T-34 with armour added on the front by STZ. Kalinin Front, 1942.

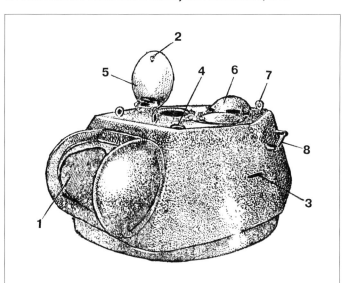

Improved turret: general layout:

1 – gun and coaxial machinegun port;	5 – hatch cover;
2 – hatch cover lock;	6 – fan hood;
3 – observation port;	7 – lifting eye;
4 – PT-4-7 sight mounting port;	8 – dismounting rail.

A T-34 with the "improved" turret operating as part of the 106th Tank Brigade. September 1942.

A T-34 mod. 1942 featuring the cast sprocket without rollers.

turret was needed, which was developed by M.A. Nabutovsky in the spring 1942. This one was called "six-sided" or "improved." Both names are not quite correct, for the previous turret was also six-sided, but a bit more elongated and streamlined. As for the "improved" in its name, this word attributed entirely to the production technology, because the new one was still very narrow and uncomfortable for the crew. By the way, tank crewmen nicknamed it "the

nut" for it had a shape close to a regular hexa-hedron.

A more convenient shape of the turret allowed making them in three stages on three different machines at once. The final assembly also became much easier. As a result, Plant No. 183 not only increased its own turret production and became able to reject the help of Uralmash in this aspect, but also started to supply other tank plants with its turrets.

The Ural Machine-Building Plant (Uralmash) joined the production of armoured hulls for T-34 and KV tanks pursuant to the State Defence Commission's resolution dated 31 October 1941. However, before March 1942 it only sup-plied shaped hull plates to Krasnoye Sormovo and Nizhny Tagil. In the April 1942 the full-scale assembly of hulls and turrets for Plant No. 183 started there, while on July 28 1942 the State Defence Committee in its Resolution No. 2120 authorised the plant to begin mass-production of T-34 tanks, and moreover double the pro-duction of turrets for the tank, because Plant No. 264 had been stopped. The plant faced many problems when mastering the production of the tank. First of all, its cast foundries could not satisfy the demand for turrets. Plant Direc-tor B.G. Muzurkov even engaged the freed capacities of the 10,000-tonne Schleman press (one of the two operational in the USSR; the other was used in Mariupol prior to the war to drop-forge T-34M turrets). Designer I.F. Vakhru-shev and technologist V.S. Ananiev developed a new turret design to allow its drop-forging, and from October 1942 to March 1944 a total of 2,050 drop-forged turrets were made by the plant, many of them shipped to the Chelyabin-sk Kirov plant. Uralmash was engaged in tank production until 1943, and then changed to assembling self-propelled artillery systems on T-34 chassis.

In a bid to make up for the inevitable loss of the tank manufacturing facilities in Stalingrad, the State Defence Committee authorised the Chelyabinsk Kirov plant to start making T-34s in July 1942. On 22 August the first tanks were rolled out of its workshops, but as early as March 1944 their production was stopped in favour of IS-2 heavy tanks.

Evacuated from Leningrad to Omsk, the Voroshilov Plant No. 174 joined the T-34 produc-tion in 1942 as soon as the design and techno-logical documentation had been handed over to it from Plant No. 183 and Uralmash.

A T-34 with a drop-forged turret from Uralmash leaving the assembly shop of the Chelyabinsk Kirov plant. August 1943.

Speaking of T-34 production in 1942 and 1943, mention should be made that in autumn 1942 their quality had been in crisis – an apparent result of the continuous need for making more and more tanks and involvement of new, non-specific plants in tank production. From 11 to 13 September 1942 a conference of tank manufacturers was convened at the Ural tank plant in Nizhny Tagil, organized by the People's Commissariat of the Tank-Building Industry. The main item on the agenda was T-34 quality. Presiding over the conference was Deputy Commissar Zh.Ya. Kotin, who supported commissariat's inspector G.O. Gutman in expressing tough criticism towards the production plants. Strangely, many of the weak points they spoke about were the same as those set forth in the Kubinka report after the trials of the three production T-34s in autumn 1940.

The criticism paid off, and in the second half of 1942 and early 1943 many improvements were made to the T-34 design. Starting in the autumn 1942 the tank got rectangular (or cylindrical on the tanks of the Chelyabinsk Kirov plant) fuel tanks fixed on the hull rear or sides. The drive sprocket with rollers was restored to the tank in November, as were drop-forged rubber-tyred road wheels. Tsyklon air filter units came in service in January and a five-speed gearbox in March-June 1943. The ammunition load was increased to 100 rounds, and a fume-extracting fan was introduced in the turret. Also in 1943, the PT-4-7 periscope was replaced with the commander's PTK-5 panoramic sight. Many other innovations and improvements were introduced in the tank, including dismounting rails on the turret. Mass-production of the T-34 mod. 1942 (an unofficial name attributed to the tank in dedicated literature) was organized at Plant No. 183 in Nizhny Tagil, Plant No. 174 in Omsk, Uralmash in Sverdlovsk and Kirov Plant in Chelyabinsk. A total of 11,461 such tanks were built prior to July 1943.

A commander's cupola entered service with the tank in the summer 1943. Noteworthy, three plants claim in their reports after the war that they were the first to introduce it – Plant No. 183, Uralmash and Krasnoye Sormovo. The fact is that the tank-builders in Nizhny Tagil placed their cupola in the turret rear behind two hatch covers to sit a third crewmember into the turret, as was the case with the experimental T-43. However, "the nut" was too small to accommodate even two crewmembers, not to mention the third one! The cupola designed by Uralmash was above the commander's hatch cover, but it was drop-forged, and rejected because of this. The die-cast Sormovo-type cupola was the only one to suit the T-34 best.

The T-34 in such a configuration remained in production until mid-1944. Noteworthy, the Omsk-based Plant No. 174 was the last to stop making such vehicles.

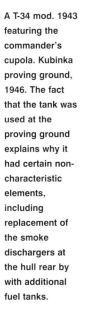

A T-34 mod. 1943 featuring the commander's cupola. Kubinka proving ground, 1946. The fact that the tank was used at the proving ground explains why it had certain non-characteristic elements, including replacement of the smoke dischargers at the hull rear by with additional fuel tanks.

T-34 PRODUCTION

Much can be said about the production of the tank. Lots of controversial publications have been available of late, with many inadequacies evident. The fact is that two-side accounting was normal during the war: plants accounted the tanks as they were assembled, and the military accounted them as they were accepted. It means that the vehicles built in late 1942 could have been accepted by the military in early 1943, and thus be included in two separate annual reports. It is known for sure that 115 tanks were built in 1940, but the army said it had accepted only 97. And so on and so forth… However, let's go down to the details and try to analyse the figures. Note, only the T-34s issued from 1940 to 1944 are listed here.

Table 1. T-34 tank production breakdown by years

	1940	1941	1942	1943	1944	Total
T-34	97	2,996	12,156	15,117	3,563	33,929
T-34 (C2V.)	—	—	55	101	39	195
TO-34 (evac.)	—	—	309	478	383	1,170
Total	**97**	**2,996**	**12,520**	**15,696**	**3,985**	**35,294**

Table 2. T-34 tank production breakdown by plants

Plant	1940	1941	1942	1943	1944	Total
No. 183 (Kharkov)	117[1]	1,560	—	—	—	1,677
No. 183 (Nizhny Tagil)	—	25	5,684	7,466	1,838	15,013
STZ	—	1,256	2,520[3]	—	—	3,776
No. 112 Kr.Sormovo	—	173[2]	2,584[4]	2,962	557	6,276
ChKZ	—	—	1,055	3,594[6]	445	5,094
Uralmash	—	—	267	464[7]	—	731
No. 174	—	—	417[5]	1347[8]	1,136	2,900
Total	**117**	**3,014**	**12,527**	**15,833**	**3,976**	**35,467**

1 – Two prototypes inclusive.
2 – All 173 propelled by M-17 gasoline engines.
3 – 2,536 tanks according to other sources. The table includes the commonest value.
4 – Including 465 tanks with M-17 engines.
5 – 354 according to other sources.
6 – 3,606 according to other sources.
7 – 452 according to other sources. This number quoted by plant, thus most believable.
8 – 1,198 according to other sources.

The assembly
conveyor at Plant
No. 183 in Nizhny
Tagil. 1942.

Turret assembly
at a workshop of
the Chelyabinsk
Kirov Plant. 1943.
The turret at the
front does not
have the mantlet
of the F-34 gun
installed.

A simple comparison of the two tables overleaf shows apparent discrepancies between them both as far as the annual production and total production of tanks are concerned. Moreover, except for 1940, all the values in Table 2 are higher than in Table 1. Why? Most likely because the reports were drafted by different executives.

Whereas Table 1 is based on the reference note "Tank production breakdown from 1 January 1941 to 1 January 1944" (available at the Central Archives of the Defence Ministry) and the information cited in "Soviet Operations during Great Patriotic War 1941-1945," i.e. represents the estimates of the military, Table 2 is based on the "Reference Notes of the USSR Tank Industry

Tanks ready for dispatch to the battle area, preparing for loading onto gondolas. The Stalingrad Tractor Works, spring 1942.

Tanks assembled by crews at gondola cars in the acceptance shop of Plant No. 183. Nizhny Tagil, winter 1943.

Commissariat on armoured vehicle production in 1941-1945" and reports of the production plants. It is noticeable that Table 2 also includes some figures filed by military representatives, e.g. the number of tanks released by the Chelyabinsk Kirov plant (ChKZ) in 1943. By the way, if 3,606 is put instead of the 3,594 in the table for the ChKZ and 1,198 for Plant No.174, the number 15,696 will appear in line with what is set forth in Table 1!

Speaking about tank production one should not disregard the information about the production of its main elements – the gun and the engine. Mention should also be made here that whereas the guns from Table 3 were mounted on T-34s only, V-2 diesels of Table 4 were used also to propel T-34-85, KV and IS tanks.

Table 3. Guns production for T-34

Designation	1938	1939	1940	1941	1942	1943	1944	Total
L-11	570	176	—	—	—	—	—	746
F-34	—	—	50	3,470	14,307	17,161	3,592	38,580
ZIS-4	—	—	—	42	—	170	—	212

Table 4. V-2 diesel engine production

Plant	1939	1940	1941	1942	1943	1944	1945	Total
No 75	477	1,933	4,295	—	—	—	—	6,705
ChKZ	—	—	173	9,115	13,868	15,292	10,895	49,343
STZ	—	—	197	2,553	40	551	728	4,069
No 76	—	—	204	5,165	6,667	7,846	5,430	25,312
No 77	—	—	—	57	2,380	4,431	3,885	10,753
Total	477	1,933	4,869	16,890	22,955	28,120	20,938	96,182

DESCRIPTION

The T-34 had a classical layout with four compartments: the driver's compartment at the front, the fighting compartment in the middle, and the engine compartment and the transmission compartment in the rear.

The driver's compartment at the front held seats for the driver and the machinegunner/radio operator, control levers, gauges and instruments, a DT machinegun in a ball mount, some of the stowage racks, the radio (not installed on some tanks of the initial series), driver's periscopes, two bottles of compressed air for emergency engine start-up, spare parts, tools and accessories.

The fighting compartment in the middle of the tank housed the seat of the commander (who was also the gunner) and the loader (who also fired the turret machinegun). The turret was mounted on ball bearings on top of the hull roof over the fighting compartment, and accommodated the main armament, some of the stowage racks and sights. An access hatch cover (two hatch covers in later series) was in the turret roof.

The engine compartment was right behind the fighting compartment in the tank's central part, separated from it with a one-piece bulkhead with hatches, covered by detachable lids. The engine compartment held the engine, two water radiators, two oil tanks/radiators and four accumulator batteries. The engine was directed to the rear, and the radiators were placed on both sides, parallel to the tanks' longitudinal axis.

The transmission compartment in the tank rear housed the main clutch with centrifugal fans, the gearbox, steering clutches with brakes, an electric starter, the final drive group and two fuel tanks.

The tank's hull was a rigid armoured box with elongated and rounded bow and rear. The hull was welded from homogeneous armoured plates, its upper sides sloped to increase resistance to kinetic-energy attacks. The main elements of the hull were the bottom plate, the glacis, the sides, the rear, the roof and the lateral bulkheads.

The bottom plate was the load-bearing element of the hull and consisted of front and rear parts connected by welding. A T-shaped beam was used to reinforce the welding seam, and was also the bottom part of the framework of the engine compartment bulkhead. The beam was welded and riveted to the bottom plate on both sides of the seam. The bottom plate was thicker in the nose. There were three hatches with armoured covers, six holes with plugs and eight cutouts, four on each side, in the bottom plate. An emergency evacuation hatch cover was in the front part of the bottom plate next to the radioman's seat.

The floor of the engine compartment had an engine seal-plate made of two lateral supports with two parallel frames fixed to them by 36 bolts. The engine was mounted on these frames.

The hull nose was made of a nose piece, three armoured plates, the driver's hatch cover and the armoured hood of the machinegun.

The top front armoured plate of the hull was rectangular at the bottom, and trapezoid at the top, and was welded to the nose piece, the side plates, the sponson bottoms and the hull roof. The hulls made at the Stalingrad shipyard (Plant No. 264) in 1942 and at Krasnoye Sormovo in 1942 and 1943 had the top front armoured

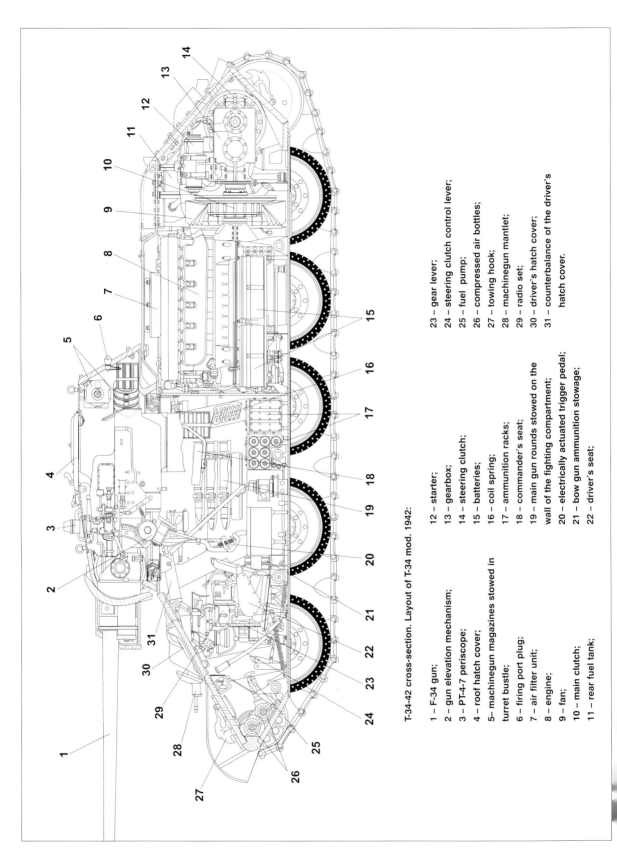

T-34-42 cross-section. Layout of T-34 mod. 1942:

1 – F-34 gun;
2 – gun elevation mechanism;
3 – PT-4-7 periscope;
4 – roof hatch cover;
5 – machinegun magazines stowed in
turret bustle;
6 – firing port plug;
7 – air filter unit;
8 – engine;
9 – fan;
10 – main clutch;
11 – rear fuel tank;

12 – starter;
13 – gearbox;
14 – steering clutch;
15 – batteries;
16 – coil spring;
17 – ammunition racks;
18 – commander's seat;
19 – main gun rounds stowed on the
wall of the fighting compartment;
20 – electrically actuated trigger pedal;
21 – bow gun ammunition stowage;
22 – driver's seat;

23 – gear lever;
24 – steering clutch control lever;
25 – fuel pump;
26 – compressed air bottles;
27 – towing hook;
28 – machinegun mantlet;
29 – radio set;
30 – driver's hatch cover;
31 – counterbalance of the driver's
hatch cover.

The driver's compartment of the T-34 tank. The driver's seat at the bottom. The black cylinder on the left is the counterbalance of the hatch cover. The TPU interphone is to the right of the hatch cover above the bottles with compressed air.

plates interlocked with the side plates, and welded.

This plate had a forged bulge for the driver's head, hinges to fasten the hatch cover and two pedestals for periscopes, slanted at 60 deg. to the tank's longitudinal axis. There was an arrangement to accommodate the central periscope of the driver on top of the hatch cover.

In early 1942 the driver's hatch cover was redesigned to feature two prism sights, borrowed from the A-43 experimental tank, and the periscopes in the front plate were dropped. Pivoting armoured lids were provided to protect the sights from bullets and fragment.

The driver's compartment of the T-34. The seat of the radioman/ machinegun operator in the bottom. The ball mount for the machinegun is in the top centre. The radio set is on the right.

Cleaning the welding seams of a T-34 hull.

The ball mount for the DT machinegun was in an armoured bulge to the right of the driver's hatch cover. In 1942 the machinegun was provided with a mantlet on its barrel, except in the vehicles built by STZ.

The sides were welded from upper and lower plates. The latter were vertical armour plates with five apertures for axle bearings, four cutouts for axle swing arm movement and five brackets with swing arm bump stops. The lubricating oil tank of the track tension mechanism was welded to the front part of the vertical amour plate, and that of

the power train was welded to its rear. The upper side plate was in fact a sponson with horizontal bottom and sloped armoured sides. Eight boxes were welded inside the lower sides (four on each side) to accommodate the slanted spring suspension of the road wheels. Oil and gas tanks were mounted in the space between the boxes.

The hull rear was made up of the sloped rear top plate, the sloped U-shaped bottom plate and two power train casings. The trapezoid rear top plate was hinged at the bottom and bolted to the sides and the bottom plate. It had a rectangular

T-34 armour diagram.

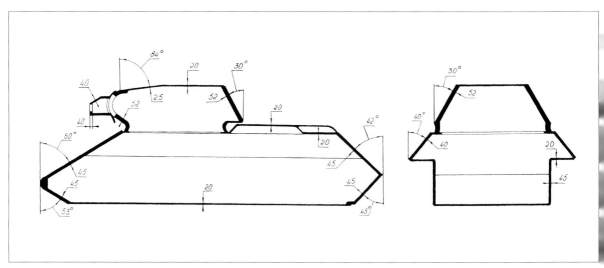

A T-34 built by STZ. Front: a vehicle with an all-welded turret and fully-detachable rear plate, fixed with eight bolts. The tanks in front of it in the column have cast turrets.

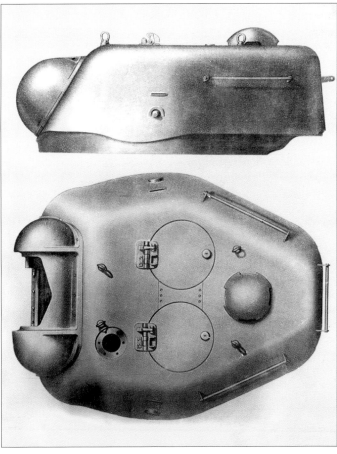

The drop-forged turret of Uralmash. 1942.

hatch cover (made round since 1942 in all tanks except those built by STZ) to access the units and accessories in the rear of the transmission compartment, and two oval holes for exhaust pipes, covered with armoured hoods.

The hull roof over the fighting compartment was made of an armoured plate with a large round cutout to mount the turret and four hatches lidded hatches to give access to the suspension springs. The hull roof over the engine compartment was welded of a top armoured plate with the engine access hatch cover, two side plates above radiators, two louver plates and radiator hoods.

The roof of the transmission compartment was made of two armoured plates covering the fuel tanks, two armoured louver plates, a narrow lateral tail plate and the grill.

The oval streamlined all-welded turret was mounted on ball bearings on top of the hull roof above the fighting compartment.

The front turret plate had three ports: one in the middle for the main armament, another one on its right for the coaxial machinegun, and one more to the left of the central port for the telescopic sight. The side plates of the turret had provisions for sights, with firing ports made under them to allow firing handguns.

There was a gun-dismantling hatch in the turret rear, its cover fixed with four bolts at first, and

The initial series of the tanks had cutouts at the rear of the turret roof to allow installing antenna. In later versions the port was welded, and subsequently was abolished at all, for the radio and the antenna port were moved from the turret bustle to the nose of the hull.

Cast turrets were also produced. Their roofs and bustle floors of the bustle were welded in place after mechanical processing, and mounts for sights were cast in one mould with the turret. These were probably all differences from welded variants.

The so-called "improved" turret was introduced in 1942, featuring a shape close to a regular hexahedron. Such turrets were both cast and drop-forged.

The sloped front of the turret had a rectangular port for the gun, covered by an armoured mantlet bolted to the turret.

Two slots were made in the turret sides, with sights installed. The turret bustle featured an aperture to mount gun a recoil test device, which was plugged from outside and fixed with a nut inside.

The 1943 series tanks had pistol firing ports under the sighting slots, also with plugs.

The turret roof was a flat armoured plate with a slot for the periscope in the front left-hand side. Command and control vehicles also had apertures for the panoramic sights in the right-hand side of the turret roof. Two round crew access hatch covers were in the middle of the turret. The bridge between them was detachable to allow fuel tank removal through the hatches without removing the turret. The hooded fume extractor port was in the rear part of the turret roof.

In 1943 some of the tanks received a cylindrical commander's cupola in the left hatch space, which was provided with five observation slots covered with armoured glass. The cupola roof, traversable thanks to a ball bearing mount, had a two-piece hatch cover with provision for a sight in one of the leaves. The tanks with the cupola did not have detachable bridges between the hatches.

Turrets of all modifications were traversed by an electric motor or manually. With electric gearing, the max traverse speed was 4.2 rpm.

ARMAMENT. The early series of T-34 tanks mounted 76-mm L-11 mod. 1938/39 guns with a barrel 30.5 calibre long and an armour-piercing round velocity of 612 m/s. The gun had elevation of 25 deg and depression of 5 deg, and its rate of fire varied from 1 to 2 rounds per minute. The weapon was equipped with a vertical wedge semi-automatic breech block with an arrange-

The all-welded turret of STZ origin. The following elements are clearly seen: the plug of the pistol firing port, the armoured side vision port with a cover attached by screws, and the PT-4-7 sight in ready-for-use position (armoured cover hinged sideways).

then with six bolts. The tanks of STZ, released in 1942, had the whole turret rear plate detachable – it was fastened to the rest of the turret with eight bolts. The Sormovo-plant's vehicles did not have the hatch at all.

A trapezoid hatch cover was hinged to the turret roof, with two ports in it – one for the panoramic periscope and the other for signalling. These periscopes were no longer installed starting in autumn 1941, and the ports to accommodate them were welded shut. In tanks built in 1942 there were no such ports any longer.

There were two apertures at the front of the turret roof – one on the left to accommodate the periscope and the other on the right for fume extraction, which was covered with an armoured hood. Vehicles built after late 1941 had two periscopes to the left and right of the fume extraction port.

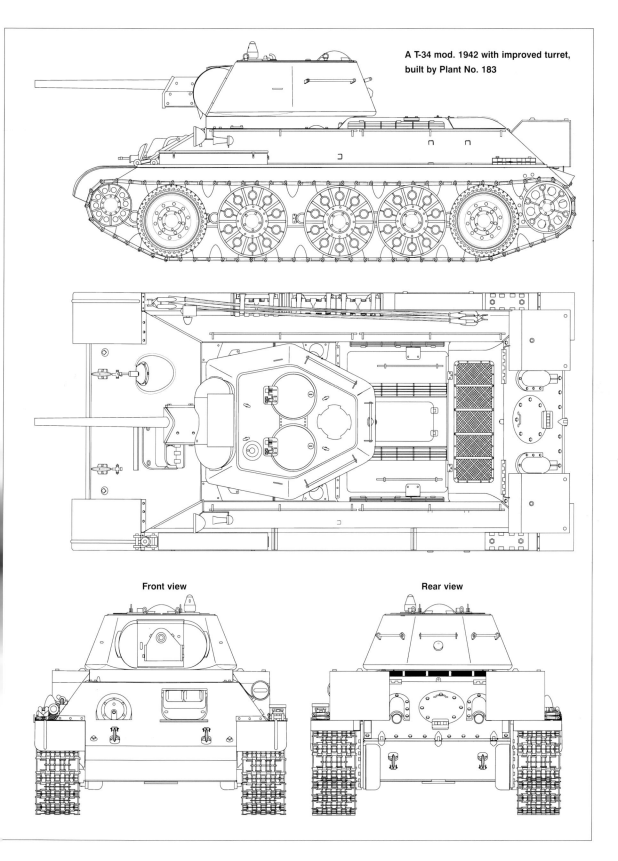

A T-34 mod. 1942 with improved turret,
built by Plant No. 183

Front view

Rear view

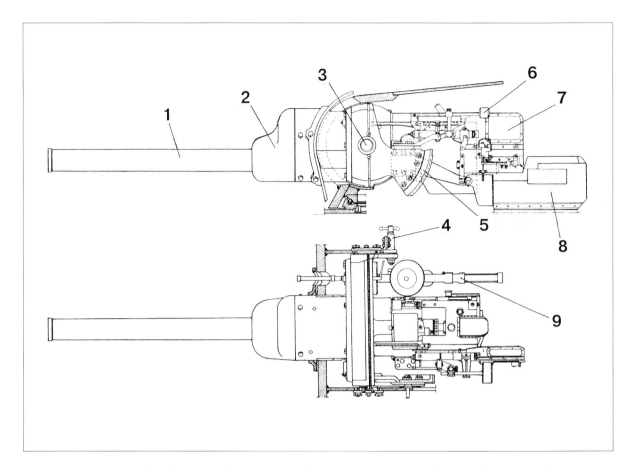

L-11 gun:

1 – barrel;

2 – mounting assembly;

3 – trunnion;

4 – travel lock;

5 – toothed elevation arc;

6 – brow pad of the sight;

7 – buffer;

8 – spent case bin;

9 – DT machinegun.

ment to disengage the semi-automatic system, because the MAAD leadership thought before the war that tank guns should in no way be semi-automatic (because this generally meant noxious fume levels in the fighting compartment).

From February to March 1941, T-34 tanks were fitted with 76-mm F-34 mod. 1940 tank guns with 41.5 calibre-long barrels, weighing 1,155 kg. The maximum recoil was 390 mm, and the elevation was 26 deg 48' and depression 5 deg 30'. The recoil mechanisms of the gun included a hydraulic buffer and recuperator, both placed under the barrel.

The trigger assembly was actuated either by foot or by hand.

The tank's secondary weapons included two 7.62-mm DT machineguns – one in the turret coaxial with the main armament and the other in the ball mount in the hull front armour plate.

When the L-11 was installed, aiming was effected with the use of a TOD-6 telescope or PT-6 panoramic periscope, while with the F-34 the more advanced TOD-7 and PT-7 were preferred. They were later replaced by the TMFD-7 telescopic sight and a PT-4-7 panoramic

periscope. Command and control tanks were equipped with the PT-K commander's periscope in addition to the original panoramic sight.

To allow the tank be used for indirect fire, an elevation level was added to the cradle of the F-34 gun.

Both weapons fired the one-piece rounds organic for the mod. 1902/30 and mod.1939 divisional artillery systems, and the ammunition of the regiment-level mod. 1927 gun, featuring:

– high-explosive/fragmentation projectile (steel OF-350 or toughened cast iron OF-350A) with KTM-1 fuse;

– high-explosive projectile of the old Russian design (F-354) with KT-3, KTM-3 or 3GT fuses;

– armour-piercing/tracer projectile (BR-350A, BR-350B, R-350SP) with Military District-5 fuse;

– shaped-charge projectile (BP-353A) with BM fuse;

– shrapnel projectile (Sh-354 and Sh-354T) and Gartz shrapnel projectile (Sh-354G) with 22-sec./T-6 tube;

– shrapnel projectile (Sh-361) and T-3UG tube;

– canister shot projectiles (Sh-350).

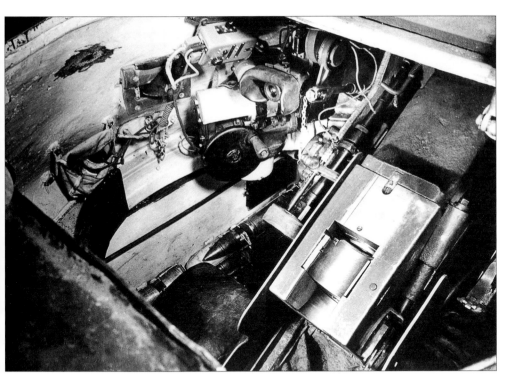

A view into a T-34's turret through the turret roof hatch. The TMDF-7 telescope is seen to the left of the breechblock of the F-34 gun. The browpad and the ocular of the PT-4-7 periscope are above, as well as the handwheel of the turret traverse mechanism. The TPU interphone station No. 1 (of the commander) is above the handwheel. To the left of the TPU is the frame of the vision port, using which, judging from what is seen in the picture, was not very comfortable for the tank commander.

In October 1943 a new round was added to the tank's ammunition, featuring the BR-354P armour-piercing discarding sabot projectile.

The ammunition load of tanks released in 1940-1942 was 77 rounds, stowed on the floor and the walls of the fighting compartment. 20 high cases to stow three rounds each and four low ones for two rounds each were fixed to the floor of the fighting compartment, their total capacity being 68 rounds. The remaining nine rounds were attached to the walls of the compartment – three on the right in a horizontal stowage rack and six on the left in two horizontal stowage racks.

The standard mantlet of the F-34 gun.

were kept in clusters on top of the case cover in the rear right-hand corner of the fighting compartment, eight high-explosive/fragmentation rounds were stowed on the left turret wall and four discarding-sabot rounds in clusters were attached to the right wall of the compartment.

The ammunition load for the secondary weapons was 2,898 rounds in 46 magazines. Earlier tank series, not equipped with radio sets, had 4,725 machinegun rounds in 75 magazines. The T-34s with the "improved" turret carried 50 magazines with 3,150 MG rounds plus a PPSh submachinegun, with four magazines, and 25 F-1 hand grenades.

Characteristics of rounds			
Type	OF-350	BR-350A	BR-354P
Weight, kg	6.23	6.5	3.05
Muzzle velocity, m/s	680	662	950
Direct armour penetration, mm, at ranges:			
500 m	N/A	70	90
1,000 m	N/A	60	N/A

The simplified mantlet of Plant No. 264 (Stalingrad shipyard as supplied to STZ).

Speaking of the mod. 1942-1944 tanks with the "improved turret," their ammunition load was 100 rounds, of which 21 were armour-piercing, 75 high-explosive/fragmentation and four discarding-sabot rounds. Eight cases were fixed to the floor of the turret to accommodate 86 rounds. The remaining 14 were stowed as follows: two armour-piercing/tracer rounds

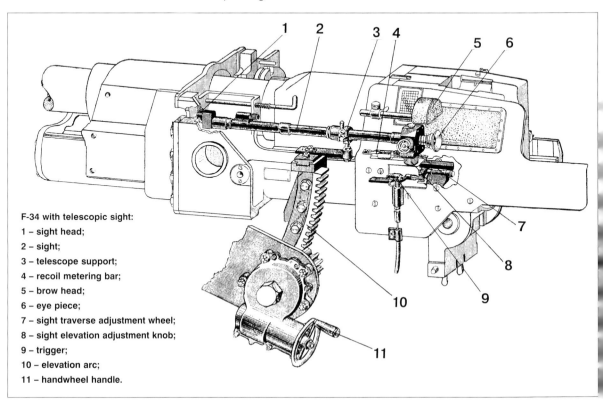

F-34 with telescopic sight:
1 – sight head;
2 – sight;
3 – telescope support;
4 – recoil metering bar;
5 – brow head;
6 – eye piece;
7 – sight traverse adjustment wheel;
8 – sight elevation adjustment knob;
9 – trigger;
10 – elevation arc;
11 – handwheel handle.

The TO-34 flamethrowing tank was armed with a piston-type ATO-41 or ATO-42 flame-throwers developed and assembled by Plant No. 222. These weapons were mounted on ball mounts instead of the bow machinegun. The incendiary fuel, composed of 60% black oil and 40% kerosene was propelled by the expansion gases resultant from the burning of the propellant charge for a 45-mm tank gun round. The flame-thrower was reloaded automatically, for which the hydraulic force produced by the fire mixture was responsible. The incendiary fuel was ignited by a gasoline torch, which in its turn was ignited by an electric spark. The flame-thrower was capable of semi-automatic and full-automatic fire (3-4 round bursts), with an effective flame range of 60-65 m. About 10 litres of the flame mixture were sprayed and ignited in one cycle. The capacity of the tank for the incendiary fuel was 100 litres (200 in ATO-42), and that of the gasoline torch can was two litres. The ammunition load for the main armament in such tanks remained unchanged, while the load of machineguns rounds was reduced to 2,750.

ENGINE AND TRANSMISSION. The T-34 was propelled by a 12-cylinder, V-60, four-stroke V-2-34 diesel, developing 450 hp at 1,750 rpm (normal rated power), 400 hp at 1,700 rpm (service power) and 500 hp at 1,800 (max power). The engine's compression rate was 14-15, and the

dry weight with the generator and without the exhaust manifold was 750 kg.

The tank burnt DT diesel fuel, or E-type gas-oil. The fuel was fed by a fuel pump. Earlier series were equipped with six fuel tanks, with a total capacity of 460 litres, plus four drum-type tanks for 134 litres in total. By summer 1943 the number of internal fuel tanks was increased to eight, so the total fuel capacity grew to 540 litres. Instead of the four side fuel tanks, two drum-type ones were introduced, and in 1943 two such tanks

A view of the T-34 engine from the turret. The filler opening of the radiator with a steam and air valve is behind the air filter assembly. Oil tanks are on the sides between the road wheel stations.

The T-34's transmission. An electric starter is mounted on top of the gearbox, and steering clutches are at its sides.

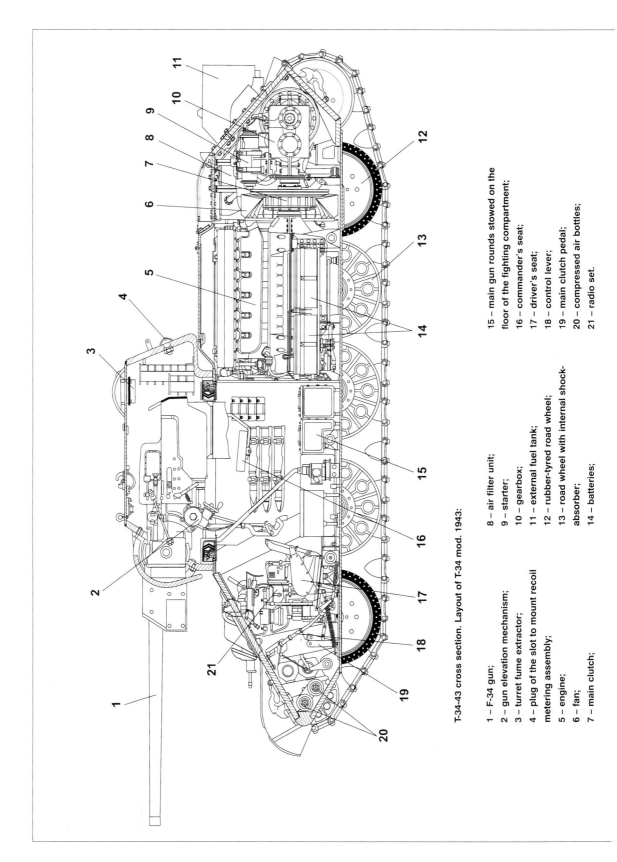

T-34-43 cross section. Layout of T-34 mod. 1943:

1 – F-34 gun;
2 – gun elevation mechanism;
3 – turret fume extractor;
4 – plug of the slot to mount recoil metering assembly;
5 – engine;
6 – fan;
7 – main clutch;

8 – air filter unit;
9 – starter;
10 – gearbox;
11 – external fuel tank;
12 – rubber-tyred road wheel;
13 – road wheel with internal shock-absorber;
14 – batteries;

15 – main gun rounds stowed on the floor of the fighting compartment;
16 – commander's seat;
17 – driver's seat;
18 – control lever;
19 – main clutch pedal;
20 – compressed air bottles;
21 – radio set.

were added on each side, 90 litres each. Soon another fuel tank was added on the right side of the vehicle. These expandable fuel tanks were not connected to the fuel supply system.

The lubricating system was pressure-fed, with oil circulation provided by a three-section rotary gear pump.

The closed-loop pressure-fed water-cooling system of the tank comprised two tubular radiators slightly sloped on both sides of the engine, with a total capacity of 90-95 litres.

To clean the air fed to the engine cylinders a Pomon air-filter unit was installed in the tank, which was replaced with the Tsyklon type air filter system in 1942.

Engine starting was by an electric starter, developing 15 hp, or by compressed air (two bottles with compressed air were stacked in the driver's compartment).

The three-pass, four-speed (five-speed since late 1942) gearbox was connected to multiple-disk dry-friction (steel-on-steel) steering clutches. The contracting band brake of the tank was covered with ferrodo. The power trains were single stage.

RUNNING GEAR consisted of five 830-mm double road wheels on each side, which differed greatly both of design and the appearance depending on the manufacturer: either cast or drop forged, rubber-tyred or with internal shock-absorbers (furthermore, STZ built road wheels with no shock-absorbers at all in summer 1942).

The tank had independent coil spring suspension.

The drive sprockets at the rear had six rollers to engage the track shoe horns. In 1942 some tanks were produced without rollers on the drive sprockets. Earlier series of the tanks had spockets with rubber tyres, and later ones steel tyres.

The cast idlers featured crank lever track tightening mechanisms, and were rubber-tyred in vehicles of the early series.

The steel tracks were assembled from either cast or drop-forged links. The earlier series tanks had tracks composed of 74 links – 37 flat ones and 37 ones with horns – 550-mm wide. The vehicles built in 1942-1943 had 72-link 500-mm tracks.

ELECTRIC POWER SUPPLY was a single-wire circuit with 24 V and 12 V voltages available. The power sources included a 1KW generator and four batteries, 128 A*h each. The electric power was fed to the ST-700 electric starter, the turret traverse motor, the fan motor, standard gauges, internal illumination, head and tail lights, the horn, the dynamotor of the radio set and the lamp of the TPU interphone.

COMMUNICATIONS. The T-34 was equipped with a 9-R shortwave simplex transceiver (71-TK-3 in tanks of the early series). In 1943 the upgraded 9-RM radio set was introduced, featuring an expanded wave band.

The initial tank series were fitted with TPU-2 or TPU-3 internal communication systems. Later, TPU-3 bisF interphones were introduced.

T-34 VARIANTS' COMPARATIVE SPECIFICATIONS

	1940	1943
Date of issue	1940	1943
Combat weight, t	26.8	30.9
Crew	4	4
Dimensions, mm:		
length	5,920	6,620
width	3,000	3,000
height	2,400	2,520
ground clearance 400	400	400
Armour thickness, mm/slope angle:		
hull front plate	45/60°	45/60°
side armour plates	45/0°	45/0°
wing flaps	40/40°	40/40°
hull roof rear plate	40/47°32'	45/47°32'
hull floor rear plate	40/45°	40/45°
hull roof front plate	16/90°	16/90°
detachable roof plates	16/90°	16/90°
bottom front plate	16/90°	20/90°
bottom rear plate	13/90°	13/90°
turret front plate	45/–	45/–
turret side plates	45/30°	45/30°
turret roof	15/90°	15/90°
gun mantlet	25/–	25/–
Max speed, km/h	55	55
Mean cruising speed, km/h:		
road	30	30
off-road	25	25
Cruising range, km:		
road	300	300
off-road	227	227
Bearing surface length, mm:	3,840	3,840
Specific ground pressure, kg/cm²:	0.62	0.79
Power-to-weight ration, hp/t:	18.65	16.2

COMBAT AND ENGINEERING VEHICLES ON T-34 CHASSIS

ARTILLERY PRIME MOVERS AND RECOVERY VEHICLES

The first attempt to derive a special-purpose vehicle from the T-34 was made right on the eve of the war. The AT-42 artillery prime mover project was drafted to replace Voroshilovets heavy tractors in service with the Red Army. The program was approved in August 1940. The prime mover, weighing 17 tons, was equipped with a platform to carry a 3 ton payload. Its V-2 engine developing 500 hp was able to attain a speed of 33 km/h with 15 tons of load attached to the tow hook. Experimental AT-42s were built in 1941, but all further development and tests were suspended because the Kharkov plant that was engaged in them was evacuated.

In 1942, some of the T-34s in manoeuvre units were reconfigured in the field to become BREM armoured repair and recovery vehicles. Turrets were removed, and an armoured cover welded on top of the turret ring with an access hatch (or a commander's cupola as in the version released in 1944) provided. The vehicles were equipped with a winch, and sometimes a crane. In 1944, such prime movers were mass-produced by tank repair plants.

BRIDGING TANKS

In November 1942, tank repair Plant No. 27 in Leningrad, following the initiative of Colonel General G.A. Fedorov, built a small batch of TM-34 bridging tanks featuring a 7.7-m metal track bridge on its top. In fact, this was a standard T-34 tank without the turret, or with the turret, but with limited elevation of the gun, which carried a metal framework, hinged at its rear. The vehicle was intended to drive into an antitank ditch, so that other tanks could cross the ditch via the metal track rails on its top. With this superstructure added the tank's employment was limited. That is why the TM-34 was never adopted for service.

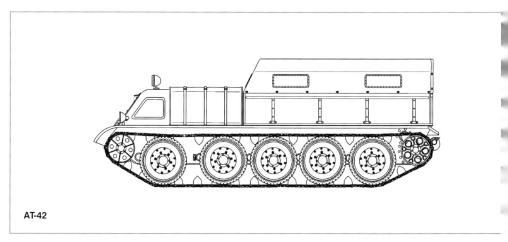

AT-42

The assembled bridging tanks participated in the offensive operation at the Leningrad Front.

MINE-ROLLING TANKS

Yet another modification of the T-34 tank was in service with the Red Army as an engineering vehicle. This one was equipped with the PT-3 (PT-34) mine roller, developed by a designer team led by P.M. Mugalev, an instructor at the Kuibyshev Military Engineering Academy, who had been concerned with the idea long before the war started.

By 1942 the design of the mine roller had been elaborated. It consisted of a number of steel wheels, interconnected to make up two banks, five wheels in each. The wheels were studded with short projecting steel girders, which applied a higher ground pressure than the tank's tracks, making the pressure-fused anti-tank mines explode. Each roller bank left a track

1,400 mm wide. The roller hubs were attached to a fork, hinged to a push bar, which was in its turn hinged to the tank hull. The roller bank assembly weighed about 5,300 kg and cleared a lane 3,600 mm wide when applied. The PT-3 mine trawl was successfully tested and adopted for service in 1942, and its mass production started at the Tula Engineering Plant in April 1943.

By mid-1943 an engineering tank regiment had been formed and first saw combat at the Voronezh Front. The regiment was organized with two T-34 tank companies and support detachments, and operated 22 medium tanks, 18 mine trawls and delivery vehicles.

FLAME THROWING TANKS

In mid-1942 some of the T-34s built at Plants Nos. 112 and 183 were armed with flame throwers. The weapons were mounted instead of the bow machineguns of the tanks. As for the appearance,

A T-34 tank equipped with the PT-3 rolling mine trawl. The Battle of Kursk, summer 1943.

A flame-throwing
TO-34 during
tests at Kubinka.
1944.

A rear view of the
TO-34 flame-
throwing tank.
Unlike manoeuvre
vehicles, the
flame throwing
tanks had the
antenna port in
the rear turret
wall.

TO-34 (aka OT-34) flame throwing tanks differed but little from the standard tanks. The flame thrower was elevated up to 10 deg, depressed down to 2 deg, and could traverse 12 deg to the right and 3 deg to the left.

Such tanks were equipped with ATO-41 piston-type flame thrower, designed by Plant No. 222. The incendiary fuel, composed of 60% black oil and 40% kerosene, was propelled by the gases expanding as a result of the burning of a propellant charge for the 45-mm tank gun round. The flame-thrower was reloaded automatically by the hydraulic force produced by the fire mixture. The incendiary fuel was set on fire with the help of a gasoline torch, which in its turn was ignited by an electric spark. The flame thrower was capable of semi-automatic and full-automatic fire (3-4 round bursts), with an effective flame range of 60-65 m. About 10 litres of the flame mixture was ignited in one cycle. The cyclic rate of fire was about 3 shots in 10 seconds. The capacity of the tank for the incendiary fuel was 105 litres, and that for the gasoline torch was two litres. The ammunition load for the main armament in such tanks remained unchanged, while the load of machine-gun rounds was reduced to 2,750.

As well as the ATO-1 and ATO-2 flamethrowers described on page 50 there was also the FOG-1 flamethrower equipment.

Apart from piston flame-throwers, tanks were tested and adopted for Red Army service in 1942 that had static flame-throwers.

COMMAND AND CONTROL TANKS (C2)

Very few of the T-34 tanks were retrofitted to be C2 vehicles, designated T-34K and T-34G. The former versions featured the RSB medium-power aviation radio set with its additional power supply pack. As a result the ammunition load of such tanks reduced to 39 rounds. As for T-34G version (stands for "General"), even fewer of them were made, equipped with the radio sets effective within 120 km.

EXTERMINATOR TANKS

Work was started in summer 1940 to improve the firepower of the T-34 tank. The 45-mm guns were no longer believed effective, and 55-60-mm ones were expected to be developed in replacement. Because the design bureau of Plant No. 92 had

A T-34 tank with FOG-1 flame throwers mounted on side plates above trucks.

been engaged in the development of the 57-mm antitank gun, it was also tasked to build a weapon of the same calibre for the T-34.

On 19 May 1941, the Sofrino firing range held the tests of the 57-mm ZIS-4 gun integrated into the T-34, as designed by V.G. Grabin. The gun was derived from the ZIS-2 antitank weapon system. A 3.14-kg armour piercing round fired from 1,000 m during the tests penetrated a 70-mm armoured plate, sloped at 30 deg. The combat rate of fire was 5 rounds per minute. However, the tests also showed the relatively weak survivability and endurance of the weapon (bore erosion was noticeable after only 100-150 shots) and poor accuracy. After the gun tube was improved, its rifling pattern amended, and a phlegmatizer was added to the propellant charge of the main gun rounds, the T-34 with the new gun was again brought to the Sofrino range for firing tests. The tests were successful and the gun was put in mass production at Plant No. 92 in July. As soon as its commonality with the F-34 was achieved, the ZIS-4 differed from the later only with a longer barrel, the wedge breech block and the counter-balance of the cradle. In September 1941 tanks with such weapons started to be rolled out from Plant No. 183 and STZ nicknamed "exterminators." However, only 42 such vehicles were assembled, because the production of ZIS-4 guns stalled.

In 1943 their production was resumed, because they appeared to be the only weapons capable of defeating heavy German tanks. In May 1943, the exterminator armed with the ZIS-4M was adopted for service. Meanwhile, four T-34 with 57-mm guns were in tests at the proving ground in Gorokhovets. They showed fairly good results, but required some flaws to be eliminated in the design of the main gun. Three exterminators were dispatched to the frontline for field tests on 15 August 1943 as part of a "Special Tank Company." Unfortunately, they never took part in combat: the 57-mm guns were tested by firing at defeated enemy tanks and pillboxes. The rectification took Plant No. 92 until October 1943, which made the guns unsuitable, because the development of 85-mm weapon was already in full swing.

A T-34 tank with a 57-mm ZIS-4 gun during trials at the Sofrino proving ground. Summer, 1941.

FIELD OPERATION AND COMBAT EMPLOYMENT

ON THE EVE OF THE WAR

The first production T-34s were fielded in late autumn 1940. However, crewmembers did not start planned combat training until the spring 1941. Unfortunately, the multiple reorganisations of the armoured forces of the Red Army during the two years' period preceding the war had a very negative impact on the training of the tank crews.

On 21 November 1939, the Chief Military Council of the Workers and Peasant's Red Army resolved that all the four tank corps existing at the time should be disbanded. Tank brigades of the Supreme Command's Reserve were formed instead, and mechanised divisions. In less than a year, the Defence Commissariat approved a totally different resolution, envisaging nine mechanised corps to be formed. Eventually, in February and March 1941, yet another 20 mechanised corps started to be deployed, but – alas – the army had neither cadre, nor hardware enough to put the plan in action. During the year

German soldiers examining a destroyed T-34. Summer, 1941. The vehicle was equipped with a cast turret, which was a rare thing, for most T-34s of the pre-war series, especially earlier ones with the L-11 gun, had welded turrets.

59

A T-34 tank of the pre-war series, bogged in a river meadow and abandoned by its crew. Western Front, July 1941. The River Drut in the vicinity of Tolochin.

and had significant improvements from the tanks of the early series, were kept in garages unused. Whereas it was insane to use BT-2 tanks to train crews of BT-7 tanks, using old T-26 vehicles in training the crews of T-34s was complete absurdity! For instance, by 1 December 1940 the tank forces of the Red Army had only 37 T-34 tanks in service. It is only natural then that proper training was impossible under the circumstances. By 1 June 1941 a total of 832 T-34s were deployed in western military districts, but of these only 38 were in use, the remainder sealed for long-storage! As a result, no more than 150 T-34 tank crews had been properly trained to operate the vehicles by the time the war started.

Different sources quote controversial opinions about the size of the T-34 fleet of the Red Army at the time the fascist invasion of the Soviet Union began. The most frequently cited figure is 1,225 tanks, built by 22 June 1941. However this is not completely correct. These are the tanks built in 1940 (115) plus the number reached by the plants in the first half of 1941 (1,110), which finished with 30 June rather than 22 June. Of these, the military accepted 97 tanks in 1940 and 1,129 in 1941. Adding one to another we get the figure of 1,226 in summary (as a matter of fact, the difference in one tank between the number of the vehicles built and actually fielded may be regarded quite plausible for Soviet statistics).

There are no uniform opinions about the exact numbers of T-34s in the military districts at the border with Poland by the time the war started. The most frequently quoted figure is 967. However, nobody kept statistics of the tanks of this or that type to the date of the war. Statistical reports were sent in as at the first day of each month. According to them, as of 1 June 1941 there were 832 T-34 tanks deployed in western military districts of the country (namely the Leningrad, the Baltic Special, the Western Special, the Kiev Special and the Odessa districts). The difference of 135 combat vehicles between the figures falls well into the number of the tanks that were fielded in western districts in June (some sources say 138).

In summary, it is next to impossible to say exactly how many T-34 tanks were concentrated at the border at the outset of the war. The closest figure should be 967. Was it this many?

By the early days of the war the Red Army had 19 mechanised corps deployed in military districts on the western border. These had 10,394

at the outset of the war some formations were formed, other disbanded, units of other branches assigned to tank detachments and so on and so forth. Moreover, the situation was developing against the background of continuous movements of units from one location to another. For instance, by the outbreak of the Great Patriotic War, only the nine mechanised corps were operational which had been formed following the summer 1940 decision. However, even these were undertrained. Training was normally organised in worn and torn training vehicles in order to save operational hours of manoeuvre tanks, which was real nonsense. As a result, the new vehicles, which often were more advanced

In retreat. A T-34 abandoned with no visible signs of damage, probably because it ran out of fuel. An abandoned BA-10 armoured car and ZIS-5 trucks. Simmer 1941.

tanks of all types and classes in the inventories (other sources say 11,000 tanks). Taking into account combat vehicles in service with some infantry, cavalry and separate tank units, the number grows to 12,782 tanks available as of 1 June 1941. T-34s accounted for merely 7.5% of the total. On the other side, by 22 June 1941 Germany and its allies had deployed 3,899 tanks and assault guns, including their strategic reserves – the 2nd and 5th Panzer Divisions (which were not engaged in the first battles of the invasion). Of this number 1,404 were Pz.III and Pz. IV medium

T-34 tanks mod. 1941 with the F-34 gun. Note that only one of five vehicles in the formation has radio sets. August 1941.

A T-34 of the 33rd Tank Brigade marching in Red Square during a parade. Moscow, 7 November 1941.

tanks, which means that 967 T-34s were quite a formidable force.

FIRST COMBAT

Unfortunately, the Soviets failed to use this force in full. Unfavourable position, absence of crews and ammunition, personnel undertraining, lack of spares and recovery vehicles disrupted the combat capabilities of the mechanised corps dramatically. During long marches to battle areas – most of the mechanised corps were deployed far from the western border – many of the tanks broke down, including brand new T-34s. Inexperienced drivers burnt out steering and main clutches, broke gearboxes and so on. It was impossible to repair tanks as they were. To make things still

For Moscow! A T-34 built by STZ in the offensive. December 1941.

Tanks of the 1st
Guards Tank
Brigade at the
approach roads
to Moscow. 1941.

worse, very few recovery vehicles were available. Only 44% of the required numbers of prime movers were in service, and most of them were used as prime movers of artillery weapons. Moreover, even where the tractors were available, they could not help much. The fact is that Red Army's standard recovery vehicles at the time were S-50 and S-65 Stalinets agricultural tractors that could not pull more than 4 tons at the drawbar. They were quite all right in towing wrecked T-26 and BT tanks, but really "kicked over the traces" when trying to move 26-ton T-34s. Two or even three such tractors were needed to do the job, which of course was often not possible.

Dmitry
Lavrinenko
(leftmost) and his
crew near their
tank. Autumn
1941‡.

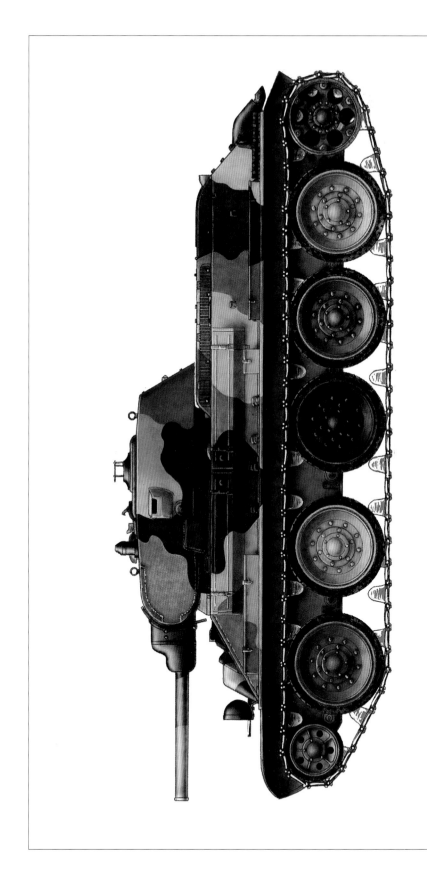

A T-34 of the pre-war series in three-colour camouflage. South Western Front, 4th Mechanised Corps, July 1941.

A T-34 built by STZ. South Western Front,
5th Guards Tank Brigade, May 1942.

Tanks of the 1st Guards Tank Brigade on the move. March 1942.

A T-34 of the unit commanded by Hero of the Soviet Union Captain Filatov being resupplied with ammunition. Western Front, 1942.

More than half of the T-34s in the western military districts were concentrated in the Kiev Special Military District (South Western Front after 22 June), while the Germans focused their main forces in the responsibility area of the Western Special Military District (Western Front after 22 June).

However, in the first days of the war the situation was developing most dramatically at the South Western Front, which is proved by the tank battle in the triangle Rovno-Lutsk-Brody that most unfortunately has received undeservingly little attention from writers.

In the evening of 24 June, a 50-km wide gap between the flanks of the Soviet 5th and 6th armies was discovered by Germany's Panzergruppe 1 with General E. Kleist in command. The Germans rushed there with 799 tanks. The threat of deep penetration into their own forces was looming over the Soviets, with the South Western Front encirclement by the Hitler troops in the North dreadfully possible as a result. To repel the aggression and defeat the attacking force the 8th, 9th, 15th and 19th mechanised corps were tasked to deliver a massive counteroffensive on the flanks of the penetrating Germany forces.

The 9th and 19th Mechanised Corps under Major General K.K. Rokossovsky and General N.V. Feklenko respectively performed an over 200-km march under intensive counter attack by the enemy aviation, and deployed for combat to the east of Lutsk with the main objective of the planned advance set to be the north of Dubno. From the south of Dubno the attacking force was the 8th and 15th Mechanised Corps with Major General D.I. Ryabyshev and Major General I.I. Karpezo in command. Mention should be made that at the early days of the war these corps were armed with 286, 279, 858 and 733 tanks respectively, which made the total number of tanks in their service 2,156! Of these 181 were T-34s and 140 KVs. However, about 50% of the vehicles were not involved in the attack for different reasons. Some were lost in combat, some broke down during the hasty march, some simply failed to come on time: the 7th Motorised Division of the 8th Mechanized Corps, for example, was still on the march at the time when meeting engagement took place. Nevertheless, at least 1,000 tanks were ready and waiting to deliver a formidable strike on the adversary, about 700 to attack from the south and the remaining 300 from the north. Most of the T-34s and KVs (at least 250) were concentrated in the northern attacking force.

On 26 June the Soviets mounted an offensive, which transformed into a meeting engagement with German Panzergruppe 1. The most powerful strike was delivered on the German 48th Motorized Corps, its 11th Panzer Division almost entirely defeated. However the Soviet forces failed to encircle the Germans, mostly because the attackers did not have any effective liaison on the ground or at headquarters. Hereunder are the reminiscences of V.S. Arkhipov, who was the commanding officer of a reconnaissance battalion of the 43rd Tank Division of the 19th Mechanised Corps at that time: "Poor radio communications available with long breaks between sessions was the reason why the information sent from the battlefield up the chain of

Hero of the Soviet Union Senior Sergeant I.T. Lyubushkin.

An "exterminator"
T-34 tank with the
ZIS-4 gun,
knocked out
during the Battle
of Moscow. 21st
Tank Brigade,
1941.

T-34 tanks in
winter
camouflage.
Western Front,
January 1941.

command was delivered with delays. The same was the cause that the decisions made at headquarters were received at the battlefield with delays, and often did not satisfy the contingency situation. For example, in the evening of 26 June, when our division approached Dubno after squashing the right flank of the German 11th Panzer Division, none of us knew that the 8th Mechanised Corps of General Ryabyshev made a successful breakthrough in the south inflicting severe damage on the units of the 48th Motorised Corps of the Germans. Moreover, the same situation repeated the next day, when all three corps – the 36th Infantry Corps, the 8th and 19th Mechanised Corps – continued to advance in the direction of Dubno. Our neighbouring 36th Corps and we were unaware that the 34th Tank Division under Colonel I.V. Vasiliev of the 8th Mechanized Corps was already in the town. It means that on 26 and 27 June Soviet forces cut 30-km deep into the flanks of German 48th Motorised Corps twice. However, the attacking forces lacked communications and liaison, which prevented them from capitalising on the success and encircling the enemy between Brody and Dubno. The encirclement was possible, which was seen from the actions of the enemy. The fact is that on 26 June, when we were pursuing the enemy, the fascists were not simply retreating, but running away in panic. Apart from hundreds of POWs that we captured, we also seized lots of their tanks, armoured personnel carriers and about 100 motorcycles, which were abandoned by their crews in running order. Approaching Dubno at dusk, the tank crews of the 86th Tank Regiment noticed eight German medium tanks that joined their column, apparently confusing them with friendly forces. Their crews surrendered at the first demand and rushed to say they were not national socialists. They answered all questions willingly. I next saw Hitler's troops in such a psychological state of panic and depression only after their defeat in Stalingrad and Kursk. This can only attest to the following thesis: the counterattack by mechanised corps of the South Western Front, undertaken on the fifth day of the war, had a real strong impact on the morale of the Nazi forces."

And not only on their morale, judging by what Wehrmacht Chief of General Staff Colonel General Franz Halder jotted down in his diary on 29 June right after the events described above: "At the right flank of our Panzergruppe 1 the Russian 8th Tank Corps penetrated deep into the rear areas of the 11th Panzer Division. This wedge must have caused real clutter in our

T-34 tanks built by STZ in Gorky Street. Moscow, 1942.

depth between Brody and Dubno. The enemy was also approaching from the southwest of Dubno which was very dangerous, taking into account the large stocks of weapons and materiel in Dubno."

Panzergruppe 1 lost 408 tanks, of which 186 were totally destroyed, as of 4 September 1941. But the Soviet losses were also immense – after the three days of the operation all four corps lost almost all their tanks. On the whole, the Red Army lost 11,712 tanks during the period from 22 June to 9 July, including almost the all T-34s.

The turret of this tank was torn off by the explosion of its ammunition. Most unfortunately, the load of 76-mm rounds used to detonate too often. Spring 1942.

A T-34 tank of the 84th Tank Brigade is advancing for combat. South Western Front, May 1942.

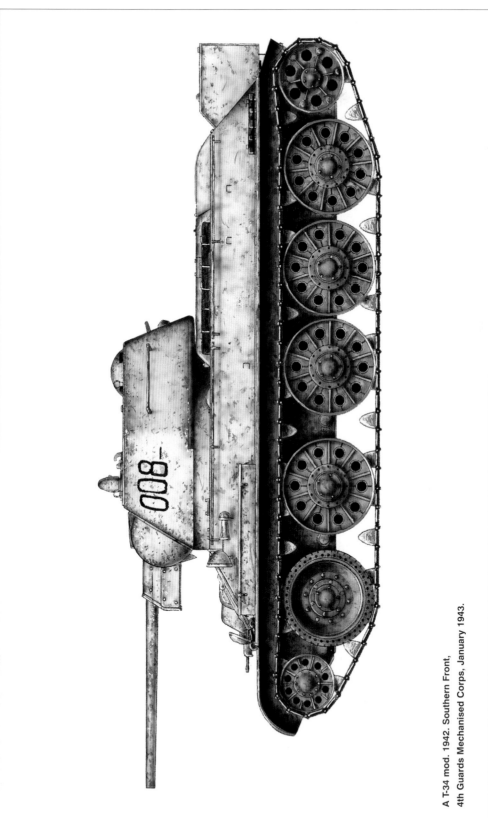

A T-34 mod. 1942. Southern Front,
4th Guards Mechanised Corps, January 1943.

These losses were irrevocable, because it was impossible to repair the vehicles as the battlefield was always captured by the Germans.

It may be worthwhile mentioning how the enemy reacted to seeing new Soviet tanks on the battlefield. Here is what German historian Paul Karel wrote in his Eastern Front: "An antitank unit of the 16th Panzer Division advanced to the front line positions with their 37-mm antitank guns. Target Russian tank! Range 100 m! Fire! The tank continued the advance. Fire! Direct hit. Another one, and one more. The serving crew continued the count: 21st, 22nd, 23rd 37-mm rounds hit the armour of the steel giant and rebounded doing no harm. The gunners were really angry, cursing at full volume. The section leader was pale and stunned. The range was only 20 m.

– Aim at the turret neck! – shouted the lieutenant.

They got it at last. The tank turned back and retreated. The ball bearing mount of the turret was rendered ineffective, and the turret got stuck, but the tank was still quite operational. The crew of the antitank weapon gave a sigh of relief.

– Did you see that? – the gunners were asking one another.

Since then the T-34 tank had been their nightmare, and the 37-mm gun, so effective in all previous campaigns, had been disdainfully referred to as the "army door knocker."

The thing that seems strange in the extract above is that the T-34 did not fire. This was either because the tank crew thought it was invincible and wanted to simply smash the weapon and its crew, which was often seen in summer 1941, or because of the lack of 76-mm rounds, which was not a rare occasion either.

By early August 1941 the active army had only 235 operational T-34s. Another 116 vehicles were in the units urgently mobilised. Immense human and materiel losses brought about a shift from the tactics of large operations to ambush techniques for which smaller formations – brigades, regiments and battalions – suited better. Pursuant to the directive of the Deputy People's Commissar of Defence dated 24 August 1941, tank divisions were disbanded to transform into tank brigades.

THE BATTLE OF MOSCOW

Brigades with different organisations of components took part in the Battle of Moscow on the Russian side. For example, the 8th Tank Brigade was made up of regiments, and operated 22 T-34, 7 KV and 32 light tanks.

The 4th Tank Brigade (Guard Tank Brigade since 11 November 1941) was formed in September 1941 in Stalingrad, and was organised with battalions rather than regiments. It was armed with 49 combat vehicles of which 16 were T-34s made by STZ. The brigade's commander M.E. Katukov led his units to success in operations in the vicinity of Orel and Mtsensk, where he was countering Panzergrupper 2 of General Heinz Guderian. The brigade was renowned for good reconnaissance and concealment tech-

Another T-34 of the 116th Tank Brigade moving to the frontline. Western Front, 1942.

T-34s of the 116th
Tank Brigade at
the start-line.
Western Front,
1942.

niques. During eight days in action it changed positions six times and destroyed 133 enemy tanks, two armoured vehicles, seven heavy weapons, 15 prime movers, an air defence battery, nine aircraft and lots of other enemy hardware. The operations by the 4th Tank Brigade are a brilliant example of mobile defensive under circumstances of significant enemy superiority.

Ambush tactics were selected by Senior Lieutenant Dmitry F. Lavrinenko, the commanding officer of a separate tank task force, when his detachment was repelling an enemy attack in Naryshkino-Pervy Voin on 6 October 1941. The threatening tanks cut through the antitank defences like a hot knife cuts through butter, came close to the positions of the 4th Tank Brigade and mounted a search and destroy operation against Soviet riflemen in the trenches. The task force of T-34s led by Lavrinenko suddenly approached them from the forest and opened fire. The Germans were caught unawares, as they

did not expect any Soviet tanks to be in their vicinity. After six Pz. IIIs were destroyed the Germans stopped the offensive and started to retreat. Lavrinenko's tanks vanished into thin air as fast as they appeared, but sprung out minutes later a little farther on the left to directly engage several more tanks. As a result of a series of such bold attacks, 15 German tanks remained unmoving on the battlefield, while Lavrinenko's task force was safe and sound.

Special mention should be made of Lavrinenko's way to immortality. He took part in 28 tank battles. His three T-34s were destroyed, but he survived. On the day when he was killed in action, 17 December 1941, he knocked out his 52nd German tank near Volokolamsk, thus becoming the record-holder in the Soviet tank forces until the end of WWII.

Commander of a T-34 tank of Lavrinenko's task force, Senior Sergeant Ivan Lyubushkin, also distinguished himself in an ambush near the Pervy

T-34s of the Stalingrad plant before dispatch for combat. August 1942. The vehicle at the front has a cast turret, the one in the rear has a welded turret.

The crew taking seats their T-34 built at Plant No. 112 Krasnoye Sormovo. Kalinin Front, 1942.

Among the greatest disadvantages of the T-34's layout was the position of its fuel tanks on the sides of the fighting compartment. The explosion of diesel fumes was so violent (empty tanks used to explode spontaneously) that tanks were always rendered ineffective. The top left side armour plate of this tank was torn off by such an explosion, for example.

Voin village. On 6 October 1941 he destroyed nine enemy tanks in two duels, for which he was conferred the title of Hero of the Soviet Union. During an action in the Battle of Moscow Lyubushkin's crew defeated 20 enemy tanks. He died in a tank battle on 20 June 1942 when an aerial bomb hit his tank, killing all the crew but for the driver, who survived only by a miracle.

T-34s in a forest ambush under the command of Guards Major I.T. Shevandin. 1942.

A T-34 in two-colour camouflage. Leningrad Front, 1944.

Exterminator T-34 tanks fitted with 57-mm guns also made their contribution to the Battle of Moscow. About 10 such vehicles were in service with the 21st Tank Brigade at the Kalinin Front. On 15 and 16 November the 21st brigade destroyed 18 enemy tanks from ambushes.

Some sources say eight T-34s with 57-mm guns, but no ammunition, were fielded with the 8th Tank Brigade of the Kalinin Front on 19 October 1941.

On the whole the Red Army units, defending Moscow did not have many T-34 tanks operational. Light tanks of old types were largely available, as well as more modern T-60s. Just for reference, the Western Front had 483 tanks in early October 1941 of which only 45 were T-34s and KVs. By the year-end the number of T-34s on the ground increased several times, but was still no more than 25-30% of the total number of armoured vehicles.

The same situation persisted in 1942, despite the increasing output of T-34 tanks. For instance, the 61st Army had 334 tanks of seven different makes in the inventory before the Bolkhovo offensive operation in July 1942. Only 67, or 20% of them, were T-34s.

STALINGRAD DEFENSIVE OPERATION

Perhaps the most violent and dramatic fighting with T-34s involved unfolded in the suburbs of Stalingrad in August 1942. It is obvious that these tanks particularly were most numerous in the tank units defending the city. The quality of the vehicles was very bad, but this did not matter any longer: until 22 August trainloads of tanks were sent to Gumrak to save their service lives. Right in the valley they were ordered to start up engines and disembark from the trains. Normally the tanks drove along the cars of the train and simply jumped off the last car. However, soon the trains were no longer needed.

On Sunday, 23 August 1942, when the most severe blow was inflicted on Stalingrad by German bombers, the tanks of the 14th Panzer Corps

A tank column on the move. A T-34 with the drop-forged turret originated from Uralmash is at the front. Kalinin Front, May 1943.

were spotted only two or three kilometres away from the tractor works, engaged in tank production. The first to be engaged in the battle were anti-aircraft artillery units, covering the factory. The crews were all women who had no experience whatsoever in laying their guns on ground targets. The German tanks simply rode over them, but by dying bravely the girls saved about half an hour for the antitank and training tank battalions to redeploy for action. All the tanks, able to move and equipped with weapons were rolled out of the workshops. Their total number was about 60. The crews were assembly and quality management shop workers. About 1,500 DT machineguns were taken from stocks and mounted on bipods. The first enemy attack was repelled.

When close quarter combat started in the streets of Stalingrad, the plant's employees repaired the tanks right at the front or evacuated damaged vehicles to the plant and returned them to the crews in mere hours. From 23 August to 13 September 1942, when tank production stopped at the plant, 200 T-34 tanks were assembled and repaired. Furthermore the defending forces in Stalingrad received 170 T-34 turrets from the plant, equipped with main guns and machineguns, which were converted to makeshift pillboxes.

THE BATTLE OF KURSK

The T-34 only became the mainstay of the Soviet tank forces in 1943. This is proved by the table below illustrating the breakdown of different types of tanks in service with the Central and Voronezh Fronts on the eve of the Battle of Kursk.

Tanks of the Stepnoy Front during redeployment. 1943.

Front	Tanks			Total
	KV	T-34	T-70 & T-60	
Central	70	924	587	1,581
Voronezh	105	1,109	463	1,677
Total	*175*	*2,033*	*1,050*	**3,258**

A tank being resupplied. Voronezh Front, 1943.

A T-34 "ironing" a German artillery battery. Judging from the position of the trails of the 105-mm howitzer its crew tried to retreat, but failed. Central Front, 1943.

The crew
mounting their
tank in an alert.
Voronezh Front,
1st Guards Tank
Army, 1943.

"Tank
dismounting"
infantrymen
taking positions
on the vehicle.
22nd Tank
Brigade,
Voronezh Front,
1943.

The tanks of the 22nd Tank Brigade with supporting infantry units break into a village. Voronezh Front, 1943.

T-34 tanks equipped with PT-3 rolling mine trawls. Kharkov operation, 1943.

T-34 tanks on the road from Zhitomir to Berdichev. 1st Ukrainian Front, January 1944.

The tanks of the 46th Dukhovitsky Mechanised Brigade moving into combat. June 1944.

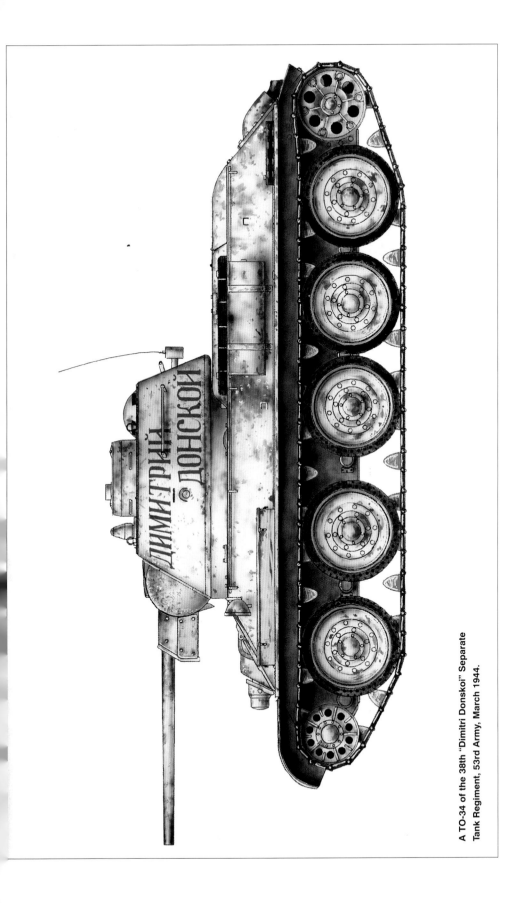

A TO-34 of the 38th "Dimitri Donskoi" Separate
Tank Regiment, 53rd Army, March 1944.

"For the Motherland! For Stalin!" The tanks and infantry in attack. 1st Belorussian Front, 1944.

T-34 tanks of the 2nd Tank Regiment of the 1st Polish Tank Brigade fording the Vistula River. 10 August 1944.

The table shows that in the tank fleets of the two fronts T-34s were dominating with 62% of the total, and of course they bore the main burden of the violent tank battles around the Kursk salient, including the famous tank battle near Prokhorovka. This battle was not like the one at Borodino, where all forces clashed on one and the same battlefield, but was actually a combination of separate tank engagements on a front 35 km wide.

In the evening of 10 July 1943, the Voronezh Front commander received the order of the Supreme Command to counterattack the group of German forces advancing in the direction of Prokhorovka. To make this possible, the 5th Guards Army of Lieutenant General A.S. Zhadov and the 5th Guards Tank Army of Lieutenant General P.A. Rotmistrov were reassigned from the reserve Stepnoi Front to the Voronezh Front. Prior to the Battle of Kursk, the 5th Guards Tank Army was deployed in the vicinity of Ostrogozhsk in the Voronezh region. It was organized with the 18th and 29th Tank and 5th Guards Mechanised Corps.

At 2300 hours on 6 July the army was ordered to concentrate on the right bank of the River Oskol. At 2315 hours the advanced guard of the Army was already on the move, and the main body followed 45 minutes later. The march war organized beyond any reproach. No movements in the opposite direction were allowed where the columns were marching in formations. The army was redeploying on a round-the-clock basis, with only short breaks for refuelling allowed. Anti-aircraft artillery and aviation effectively covered the tank columns on the march, which prevented them from being discovered by enemy reconnaissance troops. It took the army three days to cover 330-380 km. On 9 July the 5th Guards Tank Army concentrated in the vicinity of Prokhorovka. It was reinforced with the 2nd Tank and 2nd Guards Tank Corps and was tasked to set out for an attack on the German forces at 1000 hours on 12 July, jointly with the 5th and 6th Guards Combined Arms Armies and the 1st Tank Army, in order to defeat the enemy in the vicinity of Oboyany and deny him the opportunity to retreat southwards. However, the preparations for the counterattack were disrupted by the enemy forces that delivered two powerful strikes onto Soviet defences: one in Oboyany and the other in Prokhorovka.

A T-34 tank mod. 1943 with commander's cupola in the Carpathian Mountains. 1st Ukrainian Front, 1944.

A T-34 mod. 1943 of the "David Sasunsky" tank formation built with the money from workers of the Georgian Soviet Socialist Republic. 1st Baltic Front, July 1944.

Some of the Soviet forces were forced to retreat, which inflicted heavy losses on artillery units, which were just deploying for the battle or marching into deployment areas.

In early morning on 12 July a threat loomed over the 69th Army's left flank, where the Germans troops broke through the defences and were capable of disrupting the deployment of the main body of the 5th Guards Tank Army to the southwest of Prokhorovka. The enemy forces were the 6th and 19th Panzer Divisions (about 200 tanks) of the 3rd Panzer Corps, which were advancing from the vicinity of Melekhovo in the direction of Rzhavets. In this light, two brigades of the 5th Guards Mechanised Corps, a tank brigade of the 2nd Guards Tank Corps and the reserve of the 5th Guards Tank Army (tank, motorcycle, antitank and howitzer regiments) were redeployed into the defensive area of the 69th Army. These forces (about 100 tanks, including 71 T-34s) were resubordinated under command of Major General K.G. Trufanov and managed not only to stop the enemy from moving northward, but almost to repel the aggression and force the Germans to retreat to the initial positions.

At 0830 hours on 12 July the main body of the German forces, comprising the Motorised SS Divisions Leibstandarte SS Adolf Hitler, Das Reich and Totenkopf, with 500 tanks and assault weapons, including 42 Tigers, mounted an offensive operation in the direction of Prokhorovka railway station. At the same time, after 15 minutes of intensive artillery preparation, the main body of the 5th Guards Tank Army of the Soviet forces deployed for a counterattack which turned the battle into a meeting engagement, with about 1,200 tanks participating in it on both sides. Note that the enemy had more medium and heavy tanks.

Despite their surprise attack the Soviet tanks sustained severe losses to the fire of the enemy antitank and assault weapons. However, the 18th Tank Corps managed to break through to Oktyabrsky village at high speed and seized key terrain. During the further advance the corps encountered heavy resistance from a large tank group of the enemy, with 15 heavy Tiger tanks. Several hours of violent meeting engagements ended at 1800 o'clock when the corps adopted the defensive.

A T-34 tank equipped to accommodate the PT-3 rolling mine trawl in the streets of Vilnius. 1944.

The crew of a
T-34 and the
technicians of the
repair team of
Guards Sergeant
K.Ya. Yanchenko
mending the
vehicle. 13th
Guards
Mechanised
Brigade of the 4th
Guards
Mechanised
Corps, 3rd
Ukrainian Front,
Romania, 1944.

The 29th Tank Corps was engaged in a mobile combat for Hill 252.5 against the tanks of Leibstandarte SS Adolf Hitler, but after 1600 hours was repelled by the tanks of the SS Division Totenkopf, and had to adopt the defensive when night fell.

The 2nd Guards Tank Corps, advancing in the direction of Kalinin, encountered the tanks of the motorised SS Division Das Reich, which drove them back to their initial positions. The 2nd Tank Corps that was covering the flanks of the 2nd Guards and the 29th Tank Corps managed to brush the enemy aside a little, but sustained heavy losses to the fire of enemy second echelon assault and antitank weapons, and were forced to adopt the defensive.

Despite the fact that the 5th Guards Tank Army that operated on a front 17-19 km wide and had a concentration of 45 tanks per 1 km, it failed to accomplish the mission assigned. The Army's losses, not to count those of the group reassigned to General Trufanov, were 328 tanks and self-propelled artillery systems, which in total with the losses of the allocated forces reached 60% of the initial strength. The German forces lost to Soviet fire about 320 tanks on 12 July alone,

according to the report of the Voronezh Front commander. German statistics often quote a smaller count of 218 and even 190 vehicles. Nevertheless, in the evening of 12 July the German forces left the battlefield near Prokhorovka, and moreover started to retreat on 16 July. Operation Citadel had failed.

On 12 July the forces of the Bryansk Front mounted an offensive in the direction of Orel, and fresh tank reinforcements – the 3rd Guards Tank Army with 475 T-34 and 224 T-70 tanks – joined combat.

By 23 July Soviet forces managed to reach the positions the Germans had held before the attack. On 3 August the counteroffensive of the Voronezh and Stepnoy Fronts started. Tank detachments had been fully reequipped with new vehicles by that time. For instance, the 1st Tank Army had 549 tanks in its service, of which 412 were T-34s.

Later on, T-34 tanks with 76-mm gun main armament were massively used in the Battle of Kursk and later operations in the Ukraine in 1943. Mention should however be made that they were not combating enemy tanks, because there were few, but were mostly

Infantrymen
dismounting from
an OT-34 flame
throwing tank.
15th Guards
Mechanised
Brigade of the 4th
Guards
Mechanised
Corps, 3rd
Ukrainian Front,
1944.

Crews of the
Yugoslavian tank
regiment, formed
in the USSR,
during mission
briefing, 1944.

A T-34 tank built
by Krasnoye
Sormovo in
Landsberg, the
German province
of Brandenburg,
1st Belorussian
Front,
21 February 1945.

engaged in action against German antitank artillery. Of the total Soviet tanks lost in 1943-1945, 90% were lost to the fire of enemy antitank weapons and tank guns.

From the table one can see that in 1943 66.5% of the T-34 tanks were lost to the fire of 75-mm and 88-mm tank (Pz.IV, Pz.V and Pz.VI tanks) and antitank guns. In the early days of the war T-34s were superior to their rivals in terms of effective range, as they could take on all German tanks at a range of up to 1,000 m while the enemy had to come as close as 300 m to be effective. With the armour of German tanks thickened in 1943, the effective range of fire reduced dramatically and was no longer more than 500 m even for APDS rounds. Meanwhile German 75-mm and 88-mm guns were lethal for T-34s at 900 and 1,500 m respectively.

T-34 losses breakdown to fire of guns of different calibres, %									
Action period	20	37	50/L42	50/L60	75	88	105	128	Not available
Before September 1942	4.7	10.0	7.5	54.3	10.1	3.4	2.9	—	7.1
Stalingrad operation, autumn – winter 1942 – 1943	—	—	25.6	26.5	12.1	7.8	—	—	28.0
Central Front, Orel operation, 1943	—	—	10.5	23.0	40.5	26.0	—	—	—

A T-34 tank mod.
1943 in Berlin.
May 1945.

T-34 tanks during the parade on the occasion of the victory in the war with Japan. Voroshilov-Ussuriysky (now Ussuriysk), 16 September 1945.

A T-34 tank heading the parade formation of the 4th Guards Kantemirov Tank Division. Moscow, 7 November 1945. General P. P. Poluboyarov is in the turret of the tank.

It means that, by the end of 1943, the old T-34 could not match German rivals any longer and required a profound upgrade. As a result, the T-34-85 came into being. As for T-34 tanks proper, their number in the active army was steadily reducing starting in 1944. The vehicles that were still in proper order did take part in combat operations of the Red Army in 1944 and 1945, including the Berlin operation, but were generally used as training vehicles in the rear rather than frontline combat vehicles. The Soviet Army operated T-34s until the mid-1950s.

In addition to the Red Army, T-34s were employed by the Voisko Polsko (Polish National Force), the People's Liberation Army of Yugoslavia and the Czech Corps.

From July 1943 until January 1945 the Polish forces received 118 T-34 tanks, mostly from the Krasnoye Sormovo plant and repair plants. At the end of combat operations in Europe, there were still 62 such tanks in service with the Polish forces (in the 1st Tank Brigade, the officer's tank school,

the 3rd tank regiment, etc.). Some of the tanks were converted into repair and recovery vehicles and remained in operation well into 1950s.

Information is not available about how many T-34 tanks were handed over to the Yugoslavian and Czech forces. Most probably there were several dozen of them.

The Wehrmacht also used captured T-34s. For instance, the motorised SS Division Das Reich had 25 T-34 tanks in its inventory during the offensive operation near Kursk in summer 1943. The Germans fitted some of them with commander's cupolas.

There were also nine T-34s in service with the army of Finland. Seven of them remained operational till 1960.

T-34 tanks were used in small numbers by the Hungarian and Romanian armies, and the Russian Liberation Army led by General Vlasov. The remaining T-34s of the Vlasov army took part in the final battle for Prague in the early days of May 1945.

Cadets of a tank school studying the layout of the T-34 on a tank cross section. 1946.

Interoperability wargames for tank, artillery and infantry units. Moscow Military District, early 1950s.

A T-34 tank mod. 1943 during combat training at a Soviet Army unit. 1950s.

A TO-34 raised from the bottom of the Chernoye lake in the vicinity of Moscow in March 1997.

A restored TO-34 tank heading the formation during a parade of the military vehicles built at Uralmash during the weapons show in Nizhny Tagil. 2000.

REFERENCE LITERATURE

Armoured Shield of Motherland. To 60th anniversary of Main Armour Directorate. 1929 – 1989. – Moscow, 1990.

Baryatinsky M.B. T-34. History of the Tank (Armour Collection, Special Issue No. 3). – Moscow, Modelist Konstruktor, 1999.

Baryatinsky M.B. T-34. World War II Best Tank. – Moscow, Yauza, Kollektsiya, Exmo, 2006.

Baryatinsky M.B. USSR Armour in 1939-1945 (Armour Collection, 1998, No. 1) – Moscow, Modelist Konstruktor, 1998.

Burov S.S. Tank Layout and Design Calculations. – Moscow, Armour Academy publishing authority, 1973.

Chalmayev V. Malyshev. – Moscow, Molodaya Gvardiya (Young Guards), 1978.

Dorofeyev M.L. Combat employment of Soviet Army's mechanised corps in early days of Great Patriotic War. – Moscow, Armour Academy pubilshing authority, 1960.

Kardashov V. 5 July 1943. – Moscow, Molodaya Gvardiya (Young Guards), 1983.

Kolomiets M., Makarov M. Prelude to Operation Barbarossa. – Moscow, Strategy KM, 2001.

Kolomiets M., Svirin M. The Kursk Curve. – Moscow, Exprint publishing center, 1998.

Magnuski J. Wozy bojowe LWP. – Warszawa, 1985.

Materials of the Russian State Military Archive, the Central Archive of the Defense Ministry and the Russian State Economic Archive.

Muller-Hillebrand B. German Army in 1933 – 1945. – Moscow, Isographus, Exmo, 2003.

Smirnov A. Tank masters of USSR and Germany in 1941 – 1945. – Moscow, Strategy KM, 2006.

Solyankin A.G., Pavlov M.V. Pavlov I.V., Zheltov I.G. Soviet and Russian Armoured Vehicles in 20th Century (V.2). – Moscow, Exprint publishing center, 2005.

Soviet Armour in 1941 – 1945. Military-historical spotlight. – Moscow, Military Publishing House, 1973.

Soviet Operations in Great Patriotic War of 1941 – 1945. – Moscow, Military Publishing House, 1958.

Soviet tanks and self-propelled artillery systems (production versions). Album. – Moscow, publishing authority of research and training proving ground of the Armed Forces, 1948.

Svirin M. Weapons of Soviet tanks in 1940 – 1945. – Moscow, Exprint publishing center, 1999.

T-34 tank. Manuals. – Moscow, Military Publishing House, 1944.

T-34 tank. Operating Manuals. – Moscow, Military Publishing House, 1941.

Varaksin Yu.N., Bakh I.V., Vygodsky S. Yu. Soviet Armour. – Moscow, Central R&D institute of information, 1981.

Zheltov I., Pavlov M., Pavlov I. et al. Unknown T-34. – Moscow, Exprint publishing center, 2001.

Zubov Ye.A. Tank engines. – Moscow, Informtekhnika research and technical center, 1991.